"Jim Pomeroy's newest book provides a comprehensive understanding to key schisms and events within the communist world, shaping events on the battlefield. He painstakingly examines Vietnam's military history and diplomatic history and, in doing so, efficiently and effectively connects these important topics."

—Ken Rutherford, Professor of Political Science, James Madison University and co-founder of the Landmine Survivors Network, co-recipient of the 1997 Nobel Peace Prize as part of the global international campaign to ban landmines

"*Alliances & Armor* thoughtfully synthesizes the evolution of Hanoi's military strategy in the Vietnam War and beyond. It offers particularly trenchant insights on the shift to Soviet-style warfare during the latter stages of the conflict."
—Pierre Asselin, Professor of History and Dwight E. Stanford Chair in U.S. Foreign Relations, San Diego State University

"When the Vietnam War is mentioned, visions of black pajama-clad jungle fighters come to mind. In truth, Hanoi won the war by employing large formations of tanks and infantry in conventional operations. In *Alliances & Armor*, Jim Pomeroy argues that there is a direct connection between diplomacy and tactics, maintaining that the evolving alliance between North Vietnam and the Soviet Union provided the impetus for Hanoi to shift from a Chinese 'people's war' to more Soviet-style conventional tactics. Impeccably documented and effectively argued, this book is an essential addition to the historiography of the Vietnam War; it is highly recommended for those wanting to understand how and why the war evolved over time."

—James H. Willbanks, PhD, Vietnam combat veteran and author of *Abandoning Vietnam* and *A Raid Too Far*

"Pomeroy vividly describes the evolution of Hanoi's army from guerrilla bands to tank-led offensives, a development intricately aligned with North Vietnam's turn toward the Soviet Union as the war progressed. Well-researched and hard-hitting, *Alliances & Armor* examines the process that led to the war's final scene: a North Vietnamese tank crashing through the main gate of South Vietnam's Independence Palace."

—Dr. George J. Veith, author of *Black April: The Fall of South Vietnam, 1973–1975*, and *Drawn Swords in a Distant Land: South Vietnam's Shattered Dreams*

"Jim Pomeroy's *Alliances & Armor* bridges the gaps between Cold War diplomacy and military operational history. With a firm grasp of multi-archival and secondary sources, Pomeroy provides a comprehensive look at the international issues that influenced Hanoi's decisions in the Second Indochina War in a concise and deftly written narrative. This is a strong addition to the voluminous literature of the war in Vietnam."
—Kelly Crager, Vietnam Center and Sam Johnson Vietnam Archive

ALLIANCES & ARMOR

ALLIANCES & ARMOR

Communist Diplomacy and Armored Warfare
during the War in Vietnam

JIM POMEROY

CASEMATE
Pennsylvania & Yorkshire

Published in the United States of America and Great Britain in 2025 by
CASEMATE PUBLISHERS
1950 Lawrence Road, Havertown, PA 19083
and
47 Church Street, Barnsley, S70 2AS, UK

Copyright 2025 © Jim Pomeroy

Paperback Edition: ISBN 978-1-63624-536-2
Digital Edition: ISBN 978-1-63624-537-9

A CIP record for this book is available from the British Library

All rights reserved. No part of this book may be reproduced or transmitted in any form or by any means, electronic or mechanical including photocopying, recording or by any information storage and retrieval system, without permission from the publisher in writing.

Printed and bound in the United Kingdom by CPI Group (UK) Ltd, Croydon, CR0 4YY

Typeset in India by Lapiz Digital Services, Chennai.

For a complete list of Casemate titles, please contact:

CASEMATE PUBLISHERS (US)
Telephone (610) 853-9131
Fax (610) 853-9146
Email: casemate@casematepublishers.com
www.casematepublishers.com

CASEMATE PUBLISHERS (UK)
Telephone (0)1226 734350
Email: casemate@casemateuk.com
www.casemateuk.com

Cover images: (Front) Militiamen and tank troops practice how to prevent tanks from getting bogged down, March 1970. (Photographer Luong Nghia Dung; Vietnamese News Agency); (back) Victorious Viet Minh troops raise a flag on top of the former French barracks at Dien Bien Phu, May 1954. (Wikimedia Commons/Vietnam People's Army Museum System)

The Publisher's authorised representative in the EU for product safety is Authorised Rep Compliance Ltd., Ground Floor, 71 Lower Baggot Street, Dublin D02 P593, Ireland.
http://www.arccompliance.com

Dedicated to William B. Pomeroy, Jr. (1927–2017).
We miss you, Pa.

Contents

Acknowledgements   xiii
Abbreviations   xv
Introduction   xvii

Chapter 1	The Rise and Fall of a Trilateral Relationship (1954–63)	1
Chapter 2	Evolving Alliances and Shifting Strategies (1964–71)	29
Chapter 3	The Easter Offensive (1972)	61
Chapter 4	The Paris Peace Accords and the Fall of Saigon (1973–75)	81
Epilogue	From War, to Peace, to War Once Again (1975–91)	99

Endnotes   113
Bibliography   133
Index   147

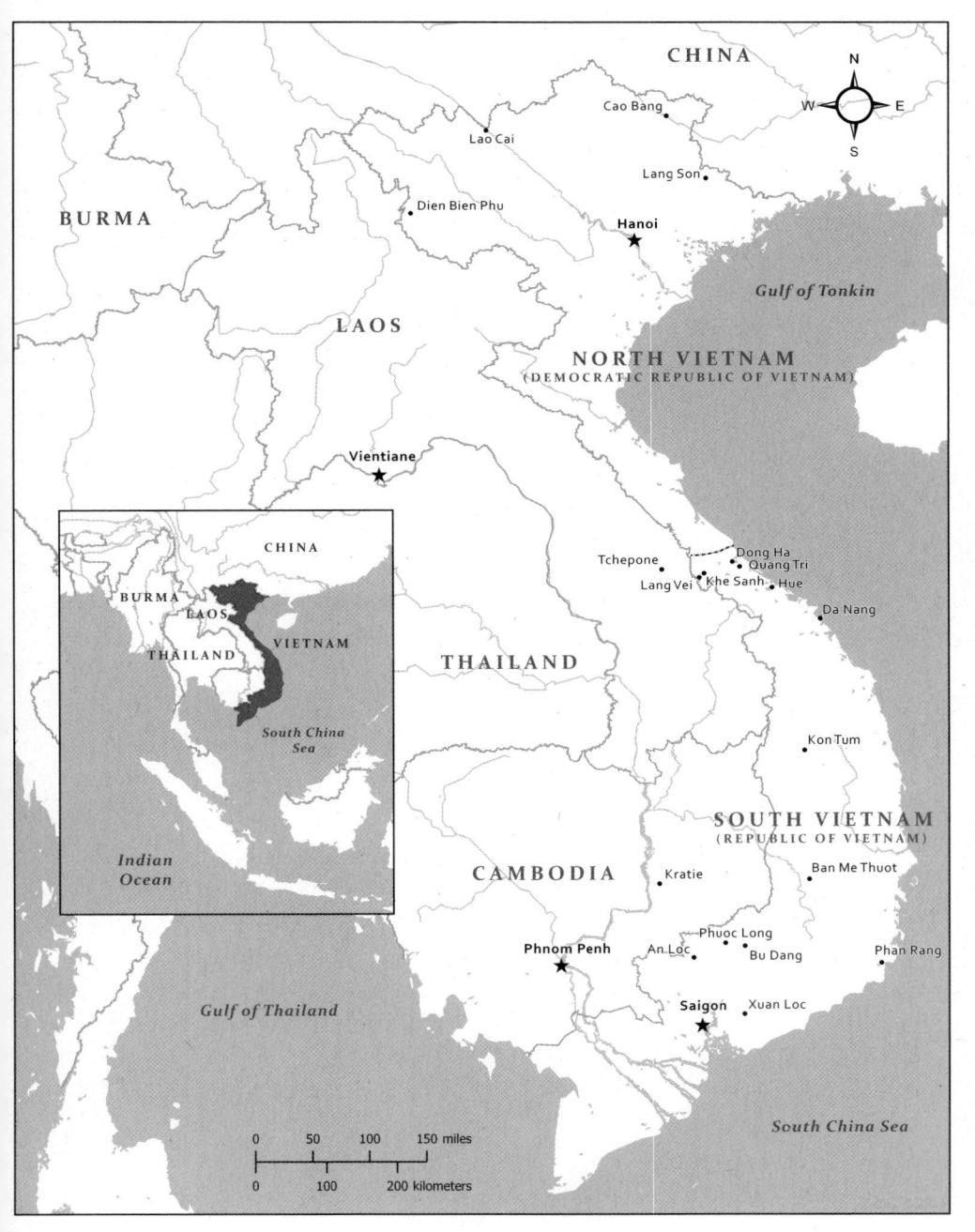

Map by Colleen Bordiuk.

Acknowledgements

Any author who is being honest with themselves would concede that it is nearly impossible to list every individual and institution that helped shape their work. First and foremost, I would like to thank Casemate Publishers and its staff for helping me publish this book. I would like to thank James Madison University (JMU) and especially Dr. Michael Galgano (JMU Professor Emeritus of History) for guiding me through my formative academic years. The life advice given to me by Dr. Galgano during my time at JMU was invaluable and helped me become the scholar that I am today. I would also like to thank Dr. Ron Milam and Dr. Justin Hart for supervising my master's thesis at Texas Tech. This thesis formed the basis of this book, and I thank Drs. Milam and Hart for their guidance during my time in graduate school. I would also like to thank Dr. Alex-Thai Dinh Vo, Dr. Jim Willbanks, and Dr. George J. Veith, all three of whom are accomplished Vietnam War scholars who helped me during my time at Texas Tech.

I would like to extend a special thanks to the unsung heroes of any scholarly project: the librarians and archivists. The Texas Tech Vietnam Center and Sam Johnson Vietnam Archive deserve a special thanks for the work they do and will hopefully continue to do long into the future. A special shoutout is reserved for Sheon Montgomery at the Texas Tech Vietnam Archive for her research guidance which helped get my thesis, and by proxy this book, started during my first year in Lubbock. Additionally, I would like to thank the inter-library loan staff at both Texas Tech and Radford University. Inter-library loans of obscure books long out of print helped inform this project greatly. Without the help of collegiate librarians, these works would have been incredibly difficult to find.

My family and friends also deserve a massive amount of credit for the completion of this book. First and foremost, I would like to thank my wife, Lauren, for always supporting my dreams and aspirations. So much so that she agreed to move from her native Virginia to Lubbock, TX, in July 2021 and then back again to Virginia in August 2023. During this project, Lauren and I welcomed our baby girl, Sophie Pomeroy, to our family. I thank both Lauren and Sophie for their combined patience and support during the late stages of my writing process.

I would also like to thank my mother and father, Jay and Beth, as well as my siblings, Joe and Katie, for their support for (and more importantly, tolerance of) my history-based nerdiness over the years. I have especially always counted my parents amongst my biggest fans. I would also like to give a special shoutout to my former college roommates and groomsmen, Liam O'Connor, Zach Archibald, and Shane Sutton. Over the years, I have counted them among some of my best friends and closest confidants. Additionally, they have always kept me grounded by reminding me periodically that "history isn't everything." I would also like to thank my good friend (and PhD candidate at the time of writing) Dave Hipple for his friendly advice, proofreading, and research assistance throughout this process. Additionally, I would like to thank Colleen Bordiuk for making the beautiful map of Southeast Asia that accompanies the text.

I would like to extend a very special thank you to my grandfather, William B. Pomeroy, Jr. (1927–2017), who was affectionately known to his grandchildren as "Pa." Pa's army stories from his time stationed in Korea—as well as the time he gifted me *Life's Picture History of World War II* when I was in 5th grade—helped shape my interest in military history, and by proxy, history more broadly. He was also one of my most passionate and steadfast supporters. Thanks to him, I think most of Clifton Park, NY, has read my JMU senior seminar paper on World War II. I miss my grandfather greatly and wish he was here for this moment. This book is dedicated to him. Lastly, I would like to thank you, the reader, for taking the time to examine (and hopefully enjoy) my work.

Abbreviations

ARVN	Army of the Republic of Vietnam (South Vietnam).
CCP	Chinese Communist Party. Governing party of the People's Republic of China (PRC).
CDEC	Combined Document Exploitation Center
CMAG	Chinese Military Assistance Group.
CPK	Communist Party of Kampuchea
CPSU	Communist Party of the Soviet Union. Governing party of the Soviet Union.
CWIHP	Cold War International History Project
DK	Democratic Kampuchea. Name given to Cambodia while under the control of the Khmer Rouge.
DRV	Democratic Republic of Vietnam. Alternative name for North Vietnam.
FRUS	Foreign Relations of the U.S. (U.S. State Department)
FUNK	National United Front of Cambodia
MACV	Military Assistance Command, Vietnam. Name of the U.S. military mission in Vietnam.
MR-1/2/3/4	The various military regions of command within South Vietnam. Map of military regions on page 56.
NIE	National Intelligence Estimate (U.S.)
NLF	National Liberation Front. The official name given to the "Viet Cong."
NVA	North Vietnamese Army.
PAVN	People's Army of Vietnam. Communist army commanded by Hanoi both before and after 1975.
PLA	People's Liberation Army. Armed forces of the People's Republic of China.

PLAF	People's Liberation Armed Forces of Vietnam
PRC	The People's Republic of China. Founded in 1949 by Mao Zedong.
RF/PF	South Vietnamese Regional/Popular Defense Forces
RVN	Republic of Vietnam (South Vietnam).
RVNAF	Republic of Vietnam Armed Forces (South Vietnam).
RVNN	South Vietnamese Navy
TOC	Tactical Operations Center
USSR	The Union of Soviet Socialist Republics. The full title of "Soviet Union."
VC	Viet Cong. The somewhat derisive nickname given to the NLF.
VWP	Vietnamese Workers' Party. The governing party of North Vietnam.

Introduction

The North Vietnamese T-54 tank rumbled down the artillery-damaged road leading towards the bridge at Dong Ha in the northern half of Military Region 1 (MR-1). The People's Army of Vietnam (PAVN), having precipitated their advance with prolonged artillery fire, was making its final attack on Dong Ha. Four days prior, the North Vietnamese had launched a conventional invasion of South Vietnam that would become known as the Easter Offensive. Unlike previous PAVN campaigns in the South, the Easter Offensive of 1972 utilized massed armored forces as a means of displacing South Vietnamese Army (ARVN) defenders, a departure from their previous tactics.

As the tank approached the bridge at Dong Ha, ARVN Sergeant Luom took aim with an M72 Light Anti-tank launcher. As one observer noted, "The spectacle of this 95-pound marine lying in the direct path of a 40-ton tank, which had no intention of stopping, was in one respect incredibly mad."[1] Luom fired his LAW, striking the turret of PAVN T-54. The tank commander then rolled his largely undamaged tank off the bridge. Remarkably, a lone ARVN sergeant had blunted a major PAVN armored attack at a crucial moment in the Easter Offensive.[2] On March 30, 1972, PAVN and Viet Cong (VC) forces launched the 1972 Spring–Summer Offensive or Ngyuen Hue Offensive (as it was called in Hanoi).

By 1972, the Nixon administration had for three years pursued a policy of "Vietnamization": The South Vietnamese Armed Forces (RVNAF) began to take over combat operations from the United States Military. Simultaneously, U.S. personnel would begin to rotate back to the States. Seeing an opportunity, North Vietnam's Politburo called for a renewed offensive in South Vietnam which would act as a final *coup de grace*. As part of their conventional strategy, PAVN (and to a lesser extent the VC) deployed Soviet-made T-54/55 tanks. For the first time in the war in Vietnam, PAVN and the VC utilized significant amounts of armored forces in the hopes of finalizing what they saw as their quest for national liberation. This major offensive, known as the Nguyen Hue Offensive to the Vietnamese, was dubbed "The Easter Offensive" by American observers.

PAVN's decision to pursue a strategy involving masses of armor and infantry in a conventional attack was not born overnight. Rather, the decisions of North Vietnam's political leadership to launch such an offense can be traced back to several key points prior to 1972. Dating back as far as the Geneva Conference of 1954, North Vietnam's considerations regarding strategy were largely intertwined with the geopolitical events and maneuvers that surrounded the policymakers in Hanoi. Foremost among these events was the constant rivalry between the Soviet Union, the People's Republic of China, and North Vietnam. During the First Indochina war, China played a much more active role in supporting the forces of Ho Chi Minh. Seeking to shore up its own regional interests, the People's Republic of China (PRC) under the leadership of Mao Zedong did not hesitate in legitimizing and supporting the communist Viet Minh forces. The Soviet Union, however, did not immediately throw its weight and effort behind Ho Chi Minh. Only after several changes of leadership, as well as the continued escalation of the war in Vietnam, did Moscow eclipse the PRC as Hanoi's main benefactor.

This book will argue that the North Vietnamese strategies put forth in 1972, including the widespread use of armor, were primarily the result of North Vietnam embracing larger, more conventional battles focused on advanced Soviet technology over China's "people's war" strategy. The widening of the Sino-Soviet split, as well as the freeze in Sino-Vietnamese relations from 1966–75, can explain, in part, why PAVN shifted strategy and began to utilize armor in battle as early as 1968. Additionally, as America escalated the war in Vietnam, the Soviet Union took a much more active role in supporting Hanoi. As part of this support, Moscow provided Hanoi with more advanced weaponry, which was something that Beijing could not supply in the numbers requested by North Vietnam.

Contrary to the Chinese model of people's war, which focused on lightly armed infantry conducting protracted war against more powerful foes, the Soviet model for warfare followed a reliance on technological innovation and superiority. In the words of Soviet Marshal V. D. Sokolovsky, "Marxism-Leninism teaches us that the basic factor that determines the development of the means for conducting warfare and of military science is the manufacture and the introduction into the armed forces of new means of combat, new weapons, and new military equipment."[3] Accordingly, the more the North Vietnamese relied on Moscow over Beijing for its military support, the more Hanoi's war began to imitate Soviet doctrines and beliefs regarding the need for advanced military technology in order to achieve strategic success. This technological approach, inevitably, led to the incorporation of large, conventional armored forces into PAVN. While the initial success of these armored forces was mixed at best, PAVN increasingly relied on larger numbers of Soviet tanks as part of its warfighting strategy. The desire to adopt a more technologically based approach to war strategy, as well as increased hostility emanating from Beijing during the latter half of the war, led to open animosity between the PRC and North Vietnam.

Another key part of the puzzle is the inner workings of North Vietnam's Politburo, and how ruthless leaders such as Le Duan pushed for a more Soviet-style conventional strategy as early as 1964. As Le Duan and his allies consolidated power in Hanoi, they agitated for more aggressive combat against South Vietnamese, and later American, forces across South Vietnam. This led to the increased role of PAVN forces engaging in conventional fights with ARVN and U.S. forces, rather than the previous utilization of local VC guerilla units in a lower-intensity people's war approach.

Lastly, the political consternations and considerations of U.S. leaders in Washington, DC, played a role in shaping North Vietnamese conventional strategy, especially between 1968–73. While the PAVN/

VC Tet Offensive of January 1968 was militarily unsuccessful, it did shift U.S. strategy to that of withdrawal rather than escalation. As withdrawal became more rapid, so did Washington's desire to reach a negotiated settlement with North Vietnam via peace talks. Accordingly, North Vietnam pursued a strategy of "talking while fighting," which eventually culminated in the 1972 Easter Offensive and the showdown at the Dong Ha bridge.

Given the multiple perspectives and angles listed above, a plethora of works have informed and inspired this book. Foremost among them is *Hanoi's War: An International History of the War for Peace in Vietnam* by Lien-Hang Nguyen. In her groundbreaking work, Nguyen seeks to examine the intricacies of the North Vietnamese government and its most powerful player, Communist Party General Secretary Le Duan. Nguyen argues that most Western literature of the Vietnam War focuses exclusively on American perspectives of the conflict, and that furthermore, "Vietnam is a country, not a war," and thus has its own political considerations.[4] Nguyen places an emphasis on the evolution of not only North Vietnam's internal politics, but its geopolitical standing in the international community. Of particular note, Nguyen places a significant emphasis on Hanoi's policy of achieving "equilibrium" between Moscow and Beijing in the throes of the Sino-Soviet split.[5]

There are several books that well delineate both Sino-Vietnamese and Soviet-Vietnamese cooperation during the Vietnam War. Two books by Xiaobing Li—*Building Ho's Army: Chinese Military Assistance to North Vietnam* and *The Dragon in the Jungle*—chronicle Sino-Vietnamese military and logistical cooperation from the beginning of Vietnam's struggles against the French to the eventual fall of Saigon. As the title suggests, *Building Ho's Army* chronicles how PAVN was transformed "from a regional army defending the North to an aggressive national and international force ready and capable of defeating the Americans from 1965 to 1973 and then the Army of Vietnam (ARVN, South Vietnamese Army) in 1975."[6] Xiaobing credits China's support for Vietnam for achieving this transformation. While *Building Ho's Army* spends most of its narrative discussing the First Indochina War, *The*

Dragon in the Jungle deals much more heavily with Vietnam's subsequent war with South Vietnam and the United States.[7]

A much more comprehensive and authoritative account of China's role in the Vietnam War is Qiang Zhai's *China and the Vietnam Wars, 1950–1975*. Zhai examines Chinese motivations for assisting Vietnam by placing them in a global context. Mao Zedong's support for the North Vietnamese, according to Zhai, can be understood as a means of promoting revolution both outside and within China's borders. Zhai states, "In sum, Beijing's Indochina policy was the result of a convergence of geopolitical realities, ideological beliefs, personality and political circumstances."[8] Similar themes of Mao's ideology and Chinese domestic policies during the Cold War are explored in Chen Jian's book *Mao's China and the Cold War*. Chen devotes two chapters to China's support for Vietnam during its independence struggle; one chapter dealing with the French-Indochina War and the other dealing with the Vietnam War. In the latter chapter, Chen spends considerable time detailing not only the evolution (and downfall) of Sino-Vietnamese diplomatic relations, but he also chronicles the evolution of economic and military aid to North Vietnam.[9]

Two works that cover Soviet-Vietnamese relations are Douglas Pike's *Vietnam and the Soviet Union* and Ilya Gaiduk's *The Soviet Union and the Vietnam War*.[10] Gaiduk's book (published in 1996) takes full advantage of the then-widely available Soviet archives to discuss the Soviet Union's involvement in the Vietnam War when it was at its height. Gaiduk decides to begin his narrative in 1964 because, in his estimation, this was when Soviet policy towards Vietnam shifted in light of the Gulf of Tonkin incident.[11] He argues that Soviet support for Hanoi during the Vietnam War was largely pursued as a means of countering China's influence in Asia.[12]

Another integral part of this book is a discussion of the Sino-Soviet split and how it affected North Vietnamese military strategy before, during, and after the Easter Offensive of 1972. One of the most authoritative works detailing this moment in Cold War history is Lorenzo Lüthi's *The Sino-Soviet Split: Cold War in the Communist World*. While this work is a very broad history covering several decades, dozens of events, and a multitude of locales, Lüthi devotes a chapter in his book to the collapse of Sino-Soviet military cooperation. In his estimation, this fallout was largely the product of conflicting advice given by both parties to the North Vietnamese as to how to best wage a war against America and South Vietnam.[13]

There are a multitude of books that deal with the Easter Offensive, as well as PAVN's use of tanks. One such book is Dale Andradé's *Trial by Fire: The 1972 Easter Offensive, America's Last Vietnam Battle*, in which Andradé levels criticisms at the North Vietnamese and their usage of tanks. A chief criticism by Andradé is that "[North Vietnamese] infantry, artillery, and armor were poorly coordinated, particularly in Kontum and An Loc. Tanks were usually sent into action without adequate infantry support, bogging down in the rubble-strewn streets where they were vulnerable to anti-tank weapons."[14] Additionally, Andradé spends a considerable amount of time describing how PAVN's shift to conventional strategy, made without committing proper thought to its supply lines and logistics, led to its inability to utilize its conventional forces (like armor) effectively.[15]

This book seeks to bridge the gaps between existing literature surrounding the Vietnam War, Cold War diplomacy, and military strategy. Most of the works listed heretofore focus on one of these aspects, often at the expense of other topics. For example, Andradé's work *Trial by Fire* does not pay close attention to the intricacies of the Moscow-Beijing-Hanoi alliance in the same way Chen Jian does in *Mao's Cold War*. Inversely, Chen pays little to no attention regarding the battlefield events in Vietnam. This book seeks to examine the relationship that domestic policies and foreign policies have on military strategies. How did the Sino-Soviet split shape PAVN's strategy in 1965, 1968, and 1972? Similarly, what effect did Nixon's overtures to Moscow and Beijing have on North Vietnamese military planning? What was the impetus, both domestically and internationally, for PAVN planners to utilize a combined arms assault involving armored formations in 1972? These are a few of the questions that this book seeks to answer. In doing so, this book will hopefully seek to highlight the Clausewitzian connections between policy and strategy.

Lien-Hang Nguyen, in her book *Hanoi's War*, has a very astute observation regarding modern Vietnam War scholarship. When discussing her research into modern Vietnamese archives, Nguyen proclaims that "it is no longer possible to write about Vietnamese perspectives on the war without consulting these materials or at least relying on scholarship that has."[16] For this book, this sentiment is true for not only Vietnamese sources, but for Chinese and Soviet sources. Given the number of languages involved and the difficulties of accessing relevant archives due to current geo-political tensions, I have had to rely on previously published works (many of which are listed earlier in this chapter) that have consulted these hard-to-reach archives and sources.

However, there are several archives that have proven to be very beneficial to this project. The Combined Document Exploitation Center (CDEC) collection at the Texas Tech University Vietnam archive has proven to be very helpful. The CDEC is comprised of captured enemy (PAVN and Viet Cong) documents that were translated by U.S. Army personnel during the Vietnam War. The CDEC contains many translated directives, reports, orders, etc., that were issued by PAVN and Viet Cong cadres during the war, and so has played an integral role in providing an understanding of PAVN's tactics and strategies during the height of the Easter Offensive.

The Cold War International History Project (CWIHP) at the Wilson Center has also provided a rich base of material for this book. CWIHP contains hundreds of documents chronicling not just the Vietnam War but the Sino-Soviet split. Perhaps most importantly, CWIHP has meticulously digitized, organized, and translated its collection, thus making it an incredibly user-friendly database. This particular archive proved to be invaluable when examining diplomatic relations between some of the Vietnam War's biggest players and personalities.

The U.S. State Department's Foreign Relations of the U.S. (FRUS) collection also contains a plethora of diplomatic documents regarding the Vietnam War (albeit from a U.S. perspective). This collection contains documentation from inside the Nixon and Ford administrations regarding U.S. policy towards Vietnam, the Soviet Union, and China. In aiding one's understanding of the U.S. rapprochement with China and the Soviet Union, the Paris Peace Accords, and the eventual U.S. withdrawal from Vietnam, this collection is first-rate.

In order to bridge the gap between a multitude of topics, a multitude of sources (both primary and secondary) need to be examined, consulted, and included. It is the author's earnest hope that this book has, at the very least, gone some way towards accomplishing this.*

---

* There is consistent debate over the use of North Vietnamese Army (NVA) or People's Army of Vietnam (PAVN) when it comes scholarship on the Vietnam War. Likewise, there is debate over the use of Viet Cong (VC) over the National Liberation Front (NLF) as well as North Vietnam (NVN) versus the Democratic Republic of Vietnam (DRV). This book will place an emphasis on PAVN when referring to the regular North Vietnamese forces. This is because the concluding chapter discusses military events after the fall of Saigon and into the late 1980s. Therefore, continued reference to the North Vietnamese Army or "NVA" would make little political or geographic sense. Emphasis on using PAVN throughout this work creates consistency. The NLF, however, will be referred to as the VC/Viet Cong (due to audience familiarity), and the DRV/North Vietnam will be used interchangeably.

CHAPTER I

The Rise and Fall of a Trilateral Relationship (1954–63)

Dien Bien Phu, Geneva, and the Evolution of Sino-Soviet Support for North Vietnam

At 1700 hours on May 7, 1954, the radio set of French Major General René Cogny sparked to life with an urgent message from his beleaguered subordinate, Brigadier General Christian de Castries. De Castries and the embattled French garrison at Dien Bien Phu had reached the denouement of their combat chronicle against the Viet Minh.* Since January, French forces consisting of Frenchmen, Algerians, Moroccans, Foreign Legionnaires, and native Vietnamese had occupied a small set of hill forts and an airstrip near the Laotian border in the vicinity of the village of Dien Bien Phu. That March, in what was perhaps a perfect example of underestimating one's enemies and overestimating one's capabilities, the French at Dien Bien Phu were quickly surrounded by Viet Minh forces under the capable command of Vo Nguyen Giap. What followed was an intense siege that saw the peasant army of the Viet Minh deploy massed artillery, effective antiaircraft emplacements, and devastating human-wave attacks against a bewildered and shocked French Army.

The transcript of the conversation between Cogny and de Castries on the evening of May 7, 1954, reads as two men working through the

---

* The Viet Minh was a nationalist front headed by Vietnamese revolutionary Ho Chi Minh that fought for Vietnamese independence during the First Indochina War. Many of its political cadres and military commanders would form the bedrock of the North Vietnamese government/military after the war.

five stages of grief together. De Castries insisted that a breakout from the encirclement was not incompatible with his command post staying behind with the wounded. However, as more and more French outposts capitulated throughout the course of their conversation, both Cogny and de Castries realized that their futile dreams of salvation were just that: futile. "Of course you have to finish the whole thing now. But what you have done until now is surely magnificent. You are going to be submerged [by the enemy], but no surrender, no white flag," Cogny exclaimed to de Castries. After briefly discussing letting his subordinate units act for themselves, de Castries said farewell to his commander: "Good, my general." Cogny replied in a rather tearful sendoff: "Well good-bye … I'll see you soon."[1] Soon thereafter, the red banner of the Viet Minh was raised over the remnants of de Castries' command post. As Viet Minh forces began to round up the 5,500 French POWs, victorious communist cadres such as Van Ky were almost dumbfounded by their accomplishment: "This was an unbelievable victory, something beyond the bounds of our imaginations. No one could figure out how we could have defeated such a powerful force."[2]

The French defeat and the Vietnamese victory at Dien Bien Phu did not happen in isolation. Nor did the Viet Minh's newfound acquisition, deployment, and use of modern weapons during the siege. Rather, foreign benefactors and allies of the Viet Minh played a large role in the ultimate ouster of France's colonial hold on Indochina. Both the Soviet Union (then under the premiership of Josef Stalin) and the newly declared People's Republic of China (PRC) led by Mao Zedong lent their support to Ho Chi Minh and his forces during the war, albeit in very different ways.

The emergence of China as a steadfast patron of an independent Vietnam was a historic moment. Since 111 BCE, China had sought to control and dominate Vietnam as a vassal state. The Vietnamese, historically, fought repeatedly against Chinese control and domination, with one of the most notable uprisings being that of Vietnamese leader Nguyen Hue in 1789.[3] Mao's China, despite having only very recently won its own lengthy and costly civil war against the Nationalist Forces of Jiang Jieshi, was more forceful and proactive compared to the Soviet

Victorious Viet Minh troops raise a flag on top of the former French barracks at Dien Bien Phu, May 1954. (Wikimedia Commons/Vietnam People's Army Museum System)

Union when it came to recognizing, supporting, and consolidating Ho Chi Minh's revolutionary forces. For example, in January 1950 (less than four months after Mao's declaration of the People's Republic), Mao Zedong became the first world leader to recognize the legitimacy of Ho's movement. Upon receiving a request from Ho Chi Minh asking for recognition, Mao sent a telegram to Chinese Communist Party (CCP) veteran Liu Shaoqi stating that Ho's request should be met in the affirmative immediately and that the PRC's "foreign ministry should pass the Vietnamese Government's statement requesting establishing diplomatic relations with foreign countries to the Soviet Union and the other new democratic countries."[4] Two weeks later on January 30, 1950, Stalin and the Soviet Union formally recognized the "Democratic Republic of Vietnam" (DRV).

The delayed recognition of the DRV by the Soviet Union and the preemptive recognition by the PRC helps illustrate a larger pattern during the First Indochina War. For most of the struggle against the French, the PRC took a hands-on approach in assisting, arming, and training Viet Minh forces, while the Soviet Union took an active yet distanced approach to its support. The same month that the Soviet Union and PRC recognized the DRV, Ho Chi Minh, Mao Zedong, and Josef Stalin conducted a series of meetings in Moscow to delineate objectives and modes of support for the Viet Minh in Indochina.

Stalin declared in one such meeting that while the Soviet Union would supply Ho's forces with a regiment of antiaircraft guns and a fleet of supply trucks, it would be the Chinese who would facilitate and implement their deployment in Indochina. It has been surmised by various scholars that the Soviet Union did not play a more active role in Indochina because of its preoccupation with Europe. In an attempt to woo France away from joining proposed Western European defense agreements, Stalin's Soviet Union often hesitated in its support for the Viet Minh. The PRC on the other hand viewed the war in Indochina as critical to its national security. As Chinese leaders watched the outbreak of the Korean War in June 1950, Mao's attention was also turned towards Indochina. His nation being a recently established communist state, Mao sought to solidify its borders in both Korea and Southeast Asia. The war in French Indochina which pitted an age-old colonial power against an upstart communist guerilla army was not only an opportunity for the PRC to pursue its nascent national security interests, but a chance for the newly christened vanguard of communist revolution to secure its own borders.

Such was the sentiment of CCP official Liu Shaoqi, who in a CCP meeting in 1950 exclaimed, "It is [our mission] to help a brotherly country for their liberation."[5] As such, the PRC was much more involved in DRV military operations than their Soviet counterparts were. Take, for example, the DRV's ambassador to the Soviet Union, Nguyen Long Bang, who in 1952 claimed that 80 percent of the weapons used by the Viet Minh were supplied by the Chinese.[6] Leading up to the decisive showdown at Dien Bien Phu, the PRC had devoted its Chinese Military Assistance Group (CMAG) to building two heavy artillery regiments for the Viet Minh in January 1953. These exact regiments would be used during the fateful siege of Dien Bien Phu one year later.[7] During the battle for Dien Bien Phu itself, CMAG advisors Wei Guoqing and Mei Jiasheng were on hand to give vital assistance and training to Viet Minh forces. The long-range trenches constructed by Viet Minh forces during the siege, which eventually enveloped French forces, were a suggestion from CMAG advisors. Additionally, CMAG provided Viet Minh forces with nearly 300 transport trucks, as well as critical medical supplies and personnel which helped treat the 9,000 wounded Viet Minh soldiers at Dien Bien Phu.[8]

Stalin and the Soviet Union, on the other hand, took a largely hands-off approach to Indochina for almost the entirety of the war. As mentioned previously, formal meetings between Stalin and Ho Chi Minh did take place. However, Stalin blatantly and obviously was not thrilled that he had been more or less forced to not only recognize the DRV, but pressured to accept a meeting with Ho Chi Minh. For example, in a telegram to Ho Chi Minh just prior to the latter's trip to Moscow in January 1950, Stalin exclaimed, "If you have not changed your plan concerning your coming to Moscow after [the publication of] the Soviet note on the recognition of Vietnam, I will be glad to see you in Moscow." Acting in a "not to be bothered" manner, Stalin's note to Ho Chi Minh exemplifies the way the Soviet Union approached the First Indochina War.[9] With the events of the 1948–49 Berlin Blockade and continued talks regarding a western European military alliance, Stalin's preoccupations pointed West, not East. To Soviet leaders, East Asia was more a less a sideshow that could and should be handled by the Chinese. The January 1950 meeting in Moscow solidified this approach to Soviet's Asia strategy.[10] Additionally, members of the Communist Party of the Soviet Union (CPSU), including Stalin himself, regarded Ho Chi Minh as a loose cannon. Having just gone through a very public and embarrassing diplomatic divorce with Yugoslav leader Josip Broz Tito, the Soviets feared that Ho Chi Minh and his comrades could become a headache as well.[11]

It took the intercession of Mao and Zhou Enlai in 1950 to dissuade Stalin of his fears that Ho Chi Minh and his movement were nationalistically hostile to the worldwide communist movement. Ho, Zhou and Mao explained, was indeed a nationalist, but "he was also a good internationalist and sincere communist who had to be supported."[12] Had Mao and Zhou not interceded, it is possible that Stalin could have very well written off Ho Chi Minh, if not downright labeled him an enemy of global communism. Instead, Stalin viewed Indochina in a neutral, essentially uninterested manner. According to historian Ilya Gaiduk, "Moscow did almost nothing to help in any material way the struggle of those [colonized] peoples, indicating that, in general, Stalin as well as his successors assigned a low priority to operations in the colonial world compared with European policy."[13]

While providing diplomatic cover to the DRV during its war against the French, Soviet material support to the DRV was minimal at best. Despite pleas from the DRV for modern vehicles and weapons in the latter years of the war, Soviet leaders such as Deputy Foreign Minister Valerian Zorin either flatly rejected these requests or concocted convenient excuses.[14] Thus, modern Soviet equipment (such as MiG fighter aircraft or the newly minted T-54 series of tanks) did not play a role in the defeat of the French at Dien Bien Phu. However, the PRC played a much more hands-on role in arming and training the DRV during the war. Realizing that a DRV victory against the French would enhance China's security on its southern flank, Mao dispatched some of his most seasoned advisors with the goal of crippling the French. As the guns fell silent at Dien Bien Phu, Chinese leaders also began to realize that this momentous victory would greatly enhance communist leverage at the upcoming peace talks in Geneva.[15]

Discussion of the Indochina issue took on a brand-new meaning at the Geneva Conference of 1954, following the conclusion of the battle of Dien Bien Phu on May 8. When news of the Viet Minh's victory reached the conference, the communist delegates present viewed the report as "literally a miracle."[16] However, within the ranks of the Viet Minh, there were some who opted for continued offensive operations against the French and their allies, though much to the dismay of the aggressive contingents of DRV leadership, Ho Chi Minh opted for the less risky approach.

The cost thus far to Viet Minh/DRV forces fighting against the French had been enormous. By the time the guns at Dien Bien Phu had fallen silent and de Castries had been marched out of his command post, the DRV had been at war continuously for over a decade. The looming specter of U.S. intervention, coupled with dwindling supplies of food and ammunition, convinced Ho to pursue negotiations with the French at Geneva.[17] One of the French negotiators at Geneva, Colonel Michael de Brebisson, also noted the precarious situation in which Ho Chi Minh and his revolutionary forces found themselves: "The population they [the DRV] control is weary of the burden of this war. Dien Bien Phu was a victory that exerted a high price. They [the Viet Minh/DRV forces] may be able to take over the Tonkin delta, but this will exact a higher price and will give rise to fresh depredations."[18] Even as Viet Minh forces tightened the noose around the French at Dien Bien Phu, Mao Zedong issued a communique to his subordinates worrying that Ho had spread his forces too thin.[19]

Negotiations undertaken by Soviet representative Vyacheslav Molotov and PRC representative Zhou Enlai ensured that the DRV would have representatives present at Geneva once negotiations began. On May 10, 1954, the leader of the DRV delegation to Geneva Pham Van Dong outlined the main points of the DRV which had been constructed according to an agreement made with Molotov and Zhou Enlai. Pham called for the independence and sovereignty of Laos, Cambodia, and Vietnam, the withdrawal of foreign troops, and the inclusion of Laotian and Cambodian communist parties at the Geneva talks. All of these core conditions, in addition to an exchange of prisoners, would be predicated by a ceasefire across Indochina.[20]

Despite the forcefulness exhibited by Pham Van Dong and the DRV delegation, it was clear to most observers that Ho's representatives in Geneva were in way over their heads. Despite negotiating in years past—such as the Fontainebleau Agreement of 1946—Ho Chi Minh, Pham Van Dong, and their compatriots had never experienced an international conference of the magnitude seen at Geneva in 1954. In addition to bringing an inexperienced delegation, the DRV was the junior attendee when compared to the other participants: France, the United States, the People's Republic of China, the Soviet Union, and the United Kingdom. The DRV stood alongside other Indochinese representatives from the Southern Vietnamese administration of Bao Dai, as well as the French-aligned royal governments of Laos and Cambodia.[21]

With such a large contingent of nations present at Geneva, one in particular garnered much of the world's attention. In what historian Frederik Logevall called "a kind of international coming-out," the PRC's delegation, under the hawkish supervision of Zhou Enlai, received an almost celebrity level of international notoriety as they arrived at Geneva in April of 1954. Refusing to share a headquarters with their Soviet counterparts, the PRC delegation sought to stake out its newfound independence and hopefully attain international diplomatic status.[22] Famously, Zhou Enlai also brought, as part of the PRC's delegation, two master chefs as a means to "make friends" during the conference.[23]

Additionally, as was often the case during his premiership, Mao Zedong sought to assert Chinese power abroad so as to enhance his political control at home. In order to launch his "Five-Year Plan" for domestic economic and agricultural advancement, Mao desired to help foment a peaceful international Cold War environment with an emphasis placed on East Asia.[24] Also, having just concluded a costly war on the Korean Peninsula against American forces, Mao did not want to see renewed American military engagement in east Asia. The sudden victory at Dien Bien Phu, while considered miraculous in certain respects, inherently brought about the possibility of direct U.S. intervention in Indochina. Well aware that some conservative voices around the Eisenhower administration still lamented the "loss of China," Mao and his chief negotiator, Zhou Enlai, entered the Geneva conference with the absolute goal of bringing an end to the conflict so as to avoid another conflagration on par with Korea.[25]

Fears of an American intervention in Indochina were not completely unfounded. Just prior to and during the talks in Geneva, the Eisenhower administration debated sending U.S. troops into Indochina. At the onset of these debates, key administration figures such as Chairman of the Joint Chiefs of Staff Admiral Arthur Radford and Secretary of State John Foster Dulles favored military intervention to stave off a total French defeat. However, these proposals were eventually considered off the table for a variety of reasons. First and foremost, as pointed out by Army Chief of Staff General Matthew Ridgeway, a large commitment of U.S. ground troops in Indochina would put American troop deployments in other areas of the world in a precarious position and would represent a "dangerous strategic diversion ... in a non-decisive theater." Furthermore, with the French defeat at Dien Bien Phu in May, a much more drastic commitment of U.S. troops would be required than what was previously envisaged.[26]

However, public pronouncements from the Eisenhower administration did little to assuage the PRC's fears of an American entry into the war. On April 16, 1954, a "high official" in the Eisenhower administration leaked comments to the press that if the French were to suffer a decisive defeat in Indochina, the United States would be "obliged to send troops there to fight the Communists." The official went on to say that the "loss of China to the Communists and the lessons learned in Korea must be kept in mind." Going further, the unnamed official declared that a negotiated settlement in Indochina would be, in essence, a victory for the communists.[27] Less than a day later, the administration official in question was identified as none other than the vice president himself, Richard Nixon. Congressional leaders from President Eisenhower's own party were caught off guard and demanded explanations. Comprehensive damage-control measures were deployed by the administration, up to and including assurances that the United States would not deploy ground forces into Indochina.[28] However, the damage had been done. Nixon's comments, delivered three weeks before the opening of Geneva discussions vis-à-vis Indochina, did little to deescalate the international tension present at the conference. Fears of an American intervention were present not only in Beijing, but also in Moscow.

Similarly to the PRC, the Soviets also had their own domestic and international politics to consider. The death of Josef Stalin, as well as the end of the Korean War in the spring and summer of 1953, opened up new avenues for Soviet policy-making. Another large-scale war in Asia which would inevitably bring about the involvement of Chinese forces was vehemently undesirable to Moscow. Additionally, the Soviets heavily weighed the considerations of the French in their approach to pursuing peace in Asia. Believing that achieving peace in Indochina could foster a rapprochement with the French, Moscow sought to bring the war to an end, regardless of political circumstances on the ground.[29]

Such was the international context that surrounded the Geneva negotiations. As talks throughout mid-May and early June failed to provide any significant breakthroughs, patience on all sides began to wear thin. Zhou Enlai and the PRC delegation had locked horns with Pham Van Dong and the DRV regarding the status of Laos and Cambodia. This bickering had caused a considerable delay and prevented the discussion of the larger elephant in the room: Vietnam itself.[30] Bickering also existed between American, French, and British representatives over a proper French exit from Indochina, as well as the fears that a partition of the region would amount to "appeasement" harkening back to the Munich Conference of 1938. To add another wrinkle to the negotiations process, the French government led by Prime Minister Joseph Laniel collapsed in a narrow no-confidence vote on June 12. Six days later, French National Assembly member and outspoken critic of the Indochina War, Pierre Mendès France, became France's new prime minister. In addition to replacing Laniel at the negotiating table, Mendès France declared on the day of his appointment that he would resign in 30 days if a deal at Geneva was not reached.[31]

With the dual pressures of Mendès France's deadline as well as the specter of American intervention still looming, the Soviets—and especially the Chinese—sought to exert maximum pressure on Pham Van Dong and his delegation to reach a deal. Zhou Enlai, representing the overall mood of the PRC, sought to move fast and achieve a settlement, even if that required offering up concessions that flew in the face of Pham Van Dong's earlier proclamations. One such concession was the status of Laos and Cambodia. DRV representatives viewed these two countries as being part of a larger Indochinese federation in which Vietnam would play a dominant role. However, Zhou Enlai was adamantly against such an arrangement. In a meeting with the Soviet and DRV delegations on June 15, Zhou proclaimed that "under the current circumstances, our side should make some concession on the Laos and Cambodia questions in accordance with our established policies, so that the conference will continue."[32]

Perhaps the biggest obstacle to Pham Van Dong maintaining the hardline negotiating stance he had earlier championed came in early July. While the Geneva conference was between negotiating sessions, Zhou Enlai met with Ho Chi Minh and other DRV representatives in the southern Chinese city of Liuzhou. From July 3–5, the Chinese and Vietnamese took stock of the most recent round of negotiations at Geneva and planned out the course of the rest of the negotiations to follow.

Zhou continuously stressed the precariousness of the current situation in Indochina. While the victory at Dien Bien Phu had been unexpected and decisive, French forces in Indochina still outnumbered those of the Viet Minh. Discussions of a continued military campaign against the French were met with harsh realities at Liuzhou. Present at the discussion was the newly victorious Vo Nguyen Giap, along with his top CMAG advisors, Wei Guoqing and Luo Guibo.

On July 3, Giap discussed with his Chinese counterparts the possibility of a renewed offensive against the French aimed at furthering the gains made at Dien Bien Phu.[33] Upon discussing these plans, Giap and his Chinese counterparts concluded that continued offensive operations aimed at forcing the French out of Indochina completely would take another three to five years. Ho Chi Minh, who feared that his populace had become war-weary, realized that such a feat would be largely unattainable. In addition to these considerations, the Chinese once again emphasized the threat of American and Western intervention if the war were to continue in the absence of a settlement at the following week's discussions at Geneva.[34]

On July 5, Ho Chi Minh issued a statement at Liuzhou that would seal the fate of the DRV's negotiation efforts in Geneva: "Now Vietnam is standing at the crossroads, either going to peace, or going to war. The main direction [of our strategy] should be the pursuit of peace, and we should also be prepared for [continuously] fighting a war. The complication of our work is that we have to prepare for both aspects in our strategy."[35] Henceforth, the DRV would accept a negotiated settlement at Geneva, even if it meant a partial partition of Vietnam, continued French presence in parts of the region, and the separation of Laos and Cambodia from Vietnam's desired sphere of influence. This news was music to the ears of the Soviet representative, Molotov, who happily agreed to support such a partition because it could further be used to buy leverage and good faith with Mendès France.[36]

The final phase of the Geneva conference began on July 10. Despite continued bickering regarding the location of the line of partition, an agreement was made on July 20 that declared the 17th Parallel to be the temporary dividing line separating the French-dominated South of Vietnam and the communist-dominated North. Vietnam, as well as Laos and Cambodia, were declared as "neutral states." French forces would depart Indochina and in two years' time, a general election would determine the unification of Vietnam. Until then "North Vietnam" (still referred to as the DRV) and "South Vietnam" (or the Republic of Vietnam, or RVN) would remain two distinct entities.[37]

Despite such a "miraculous" victory at Dien Bien Phu in May, the Geneva Accords formally signed on July 21, 1954, were a far cry from the initial desires of the DRV negotiators. Shortly before the final agreement was reached, Pham Van Dong allegedly expressed his frustrations with Zhou Enlai to an aide: "He has double crossed us."[38] While somewhat harsh, there is some truth to these angry sentiments. As has previously been discussed, the Soviet Union was not the primary player at Geneva on the communist negotiating side. For the Soviets, Indochina in 1954 was viewed as a problem rather than an opportunity. Events in Europe and in Moscow itself were of larger importance to Nikita Khrushchev, the soon-to-be leader of the Union of Soviet Socialist Republics. Moscow instead used the PRC as a proxy to take the lead in Geneva, a role which Zhou Enlai and his colleagues were more than happy to fill.[39]

The real winners of the Geneva conference turned out to be Zhou Enlai and the PRC. The partition of Vietnam helped prevent another major war in Asia between China and Western powers while simultaneously creating a communist-led northern half of Vietnam which would act as a buffer protecting the PRC's southern flank. Additionally, in the eyes of Mao Zedong, the PRC's involvement and success at the Geneva negotiations marked the first time since the mid-19th century that China had been accepted and respected on an international stage. Zhou's discussions and relationship-building at Geneva with Western leaders, such as French Prime Minister Mendès France and British Foreign Secretary Anthony Eden, helped chip away at the PRC's international isolation that had plagued Mao's efforts since his communist victory in 1949.[40]

Perhaps this newfound diplomatic success is best embodied in a telegram sent from Zhou Enlai to Mao Zedong on July 22, 1954, just after the Geneva Agreement had been reached. In the telegram, Zhou describes his final meetings with Mendès France and Eden. According to Zhou, Anthony Eden "said that Britain placed a lot of emphasis on the connections that had been established between China and Britain and hoped that the two countries would maintain this relationship with confidence in the future." Two hours later, Mendès France told Zhou that Geneva had been successful largely due to the PRC's involvement and that it had opened the door to future Chinese-French relations. The telegram ends with a description of a Sino-Soviet-Vietnamese celebratory dinner. In a manner perhaps rather illustrative of the entirety of the conference, Molotov declined to attend.[41]

While the Vietnamese also feared a war-weary populace and possible American intervention, bitterness existed amongst various members of the Vietnamese Workers' Party (VWP). One such party member, Le Duan, exemplified the thoughts of many of his comrades:

> Why, if Dien Bien Phu was such a massive victory didn't the party continue the struggle for a few more months in order to gain better terms at the negotiating table? Did the Soviet Union and China pressure us to sign the agreement? Why did we agree on a temporary division at the seventeenth parallel instead of a ceasefire in place?[42]

The historiography surrounding the Geneva Conference more or less confirms the skepticism and incredulity expressed by Le Duan. Historian Pierre Asselin states that "support for [DRV] positions by both Moscow and Beijing was less than stellar." The objective for both the PRC and Soviet Union at the outset of Geneva was to achieve a deal that brought peace of some kind to Indochina, not a deal that would help maximize the gains that the DRV had fought so ferociously for.[43]

The final settlement at Geneva also seemed to widen existing gaps in the DRV-PRC relationship. Despite providing significant material and advisory support for the DRV during its war with France, there was a steady drumbeat of criticism between PRC advisors and their DRV comrades. One advisor stated that Vo Nguyen Giap was "slippery and not very upright and honest." Some CMAG advisors expressed open contempt for their DRV advisees. CMAG advisor Chen Geng wrote that he found many of the DRV's cadres to be arrogant and lacking "Bolshevist self-criticism."[44] The bickering at Geneva only worsened these feelings of arrogance, chauvinism, and patronization between the newly christened state of DRV and the PRC.

While it seems that Ho Chi Minh had little choice but to accept the terms of Geneva in 1954, tensions continued to simmer within the ranks of the VWP over what was seen as a capitulation. Fourteen years later, when North Vietnam began to explore peace talks with the United States, Geneva was flatly rejected by DRV officials as a potential negotiating location due to its painful historical memory.[45]

The Sino-Soviet Split (1956–63)

As the tensions of Geneva still hung over the newly independent nations of Laos, Cambodia, the Democratic Republic of Vietnam, and the Republic of Vietnam, events in the wider communist world continued apace with grave consequences for all its member nations. Foremost among these events was the beginning of what scholars have called the Sino-Soviet split. After the founding of the PRC in 1949, Mao Zedong entered into a formal alliance with Josef Stalin's Soviet Union. On February 14, 1950, the Soviet Union and PRC signed the Sino-Soviet Friendship, Alliance, and Mutual Assistance Treaty which was specifically aimed against "Japanese militarism and its allies," namely the United States. While Mao had held quiet skepticisms about the Soviet Union's perceived apathy towards Chinese politics and "imperialist" policies towards Eastern Europe, he nonetheless cozied up to Stalin as a means of countering the more overt imperialism of the United States. However, Mao's partnership with the Soviet Union was sought after with the understanding that *"zili gengsheng,"* or self-reliance, would be needed within the PRC going forward.[46]

Two years after Geneva, the Soviet Union had gone through massive changes. A year prior to the final settlement that split Indochina, Josef Stalin died in his dacha from a stroke. In his wake, a power vacuum emerged within the halls of the Soviet Politburo and there was uncertainty as to who would take Stalin's place. Following a contentious and short-lived tenure as head of state, Georgy Malenkov was ousted and replaced by Nikita Khrushchev in 1955.[47] In a speech to the Communist Party of the Soviet Union (CPSU) on February 25, 1956, Khrushchev managed to shake the communist world to its foundations. The speech was entitled "On the Cult of Personality and Its Consequences," but was more commonly referred to as "Khrushchev's Secret Speech." In it, the Soviet leader inaugurated what became known as "de-Stalinization." To Khrushchev, Josef Stalin's reign over the Soviet Union was fraught with a multitude of problems that did more harm than good to the internationalist communist cause. Stalin's purges and heavy handedness, according to Khrushchev, "ignored the norms of party life and trampled on the Leninist principle of collective party leadership." Going further, Khrushchev denounced Stalin's harsh foreign policy towards nations within the communist camp. In a final denunciation of the Soviet Union's longest-standing leader, Khrushchev proclaimed: "We should know the limits; we should not give ammunition to the enemy; we should not wash our dirty linen before their eyes. I think that the delegates to the congress will understand and assess properly all these proposals." The end of his speech was reportedly met with thunderous applause from those present.[48]

"The Secret Speech" had profound consequences throughout the communist world; the snowball effect Khrushchev's speech had on Sino-Soviet relations was the most significant of them. For Mao, criticism of Stalin was not unheard of. As previously mentioned, Mao believed that the Soviet Union under Stalin had often dismissed the overtures and desires of newly emerging communist states such as the PRC. For Mao, Stalin did not seek to assist or formally welcome the PRC into the communist fold until Chinese volunteer forces were deployed into Korea in 1950. Furthermore, Stalin had misjudged and misinformed Mao and his comrades during both the Second World War and the Chinese Civil War.

However, Mao still regarded Stalin as a "great Marxist-Leninist revolutionary leader" and urged his fellow CCP members to judge Stalin on his historical merit rather than solely his mistakes. This stark contrast to Khruschev's blistering criticism was largely due to the fact that the PRC had already adopted a Stalinist model, especially when it came to personality cults. Mao sought to solidify China's "continuous revolution" under a personality cult headed by himself. While eager to take up the mantle of some criticisms of Stalin, the most important criticism Khrushchev levelled at him in his speech was not among those Mao was willing to embrace. Mao, and by proxy the CCP, would adopt a "seventy–thirty ratio" with regards to the memory of Josef Stalin; seventy percent correct, thirty percent incorrect.[49]

While the Secret Speech of 1956 opened the door towards declining Sino-Soviet relations, the events of that fall burst the door wide-open. A month after the speech, the Warsaw Pact member nation of Poland began to embrace some of the criticisms and tenets of Khrushchev's words and attempted to forge its own political path forward. The sudden death of First Secretary Boleslaw Bierut in March 1956 and the succession of Wladyslaw Gomulka (a Soviet critic) to the height of Polish Communist Party leadership alarmed Khrushchev and the Soviet Politburo. These fears were only exacerbated when workers in Poznan went on strike in June and the Polish Politburo resigned in its entirety in October amid proposals for reform from Gomulka.[50] Subsequently, debate within the Soviet Politburo began to circle around potential military action in Poland and placing Red Army troops in Eastern Europe on high alert.[51]

Chinese diplomats present in Eastern Europe became increasingly alarmed at Soviet saber-rattling with regards to Poland. When word reached Beijing that Khrushchev had debated launching a military operation into Poland to quell nascent anti-Soviet sentiments, Mao decried the proposal, citing Khruschev's own hypocrisy: "Khrushchev criticized Stalin's policy towards Yugoslavia as incorrect, but his policy toward Poland is even more terrible than Stalin's.... If the Soviet Union dispatches troops, we will support Poland."[52] While a last-minute visit to Moscow on October 23 by a CCP delegation headed by Liu Shaoqi prevented a full-scale Soviet intervention, the Polish crisis deepened the rift between the Soviets and Chinese.[53]

As events in Poland unfolded, Hungary underwent a full-fledged revolution that further eroded solidarity and consensus in the communist world. Following the Secret Speech, the prime minister of Hungary, Matyas Rakosi, was faced with increasing calls from his own party as well as the Hungarian populace for reform. As events in Poland reached a fever pitch in October, Hungarian protesters calling for reform were shot by Hungarian State Security Forces.[54] Watching events unfold in Budapest, Chinese diplomatic personnel were shocked and confused as to how to respond to increasing bouts of violence that threatened to tear Hungary apart.[55]

The Chinese response to these events was eventually shaped by the massive Soviet military intervention into Hungary several days after the initial street clashes. While supporting the Poles and Hungarians on the one hand by suggesting that both nations follow the "Yugoslav model" with regards to their relations with Moscow, Chinese officials such as Zhou Enlai were not afraid to call various elements of the Polish and Hungarian protests deviationists and rightists. Such was the case in a conversation between Zhou and the Hungarian ambassador to China, in which Zhou explicitly warned that Hungary should not deviate from the "socialist camp."[56]

Simultaneously however, the PRC blamed Khrushchev's "zig-zagging" and "great power chauvinism" for causing both of the revolts in Poland and Hungary. For Mao and his comrades in the CCP, the rifts created by Khrushchev's Secret Speech and the subsequent heavy-handed Soviet reactions to inevitable criticisms within the socialist camp had threatened the unity (real or perceived) of the world's communist nations. More importantly, the PRC began to believe that it was their actions alone in the tumultuous fall of 1956 that saved and salvaged the socialist camp.[57] Four years later, as the growing rift between the Soviet Union and China worsened, PRC officials would continue to remind themselves and others that they stood fast in the face of increased Soviet meddling in the affairs of other nations.[58]

While the events of 1956 opened a rift between the Soviet Union and the PRC, the events of the next seven years widened the rift to the point of a complete deterioration of relations. In 1958, Mao launched "The Great Leap Forward" in an attempt to propel the PRC ahead of the Soviet Union in terms of agricultural and industrial output. While originally a part of Mao's "left turn" in PRC politics, the Great Leap Forward would result in two devastating outcomes.[59] First, according to renowned China scholar Frank Dikötter, the Great Leap Forward caused the deaths of some 45 million of Mao's countrymen through agricultural mismanagement and subsequent widespread famine, as well as party purges.[60] Second, the hubris endemic within the goals and aims of the Great Leap Forward irritated Soviet advisors present in China as well as Khrushchev himself. Additionally, that same year, China launched artillery barrages at Taiwan which heightened tensions between the United States, the PRC, and the Soviet Union.

This brief crisis in the Taiwan Strait was a direct repudiation of the new Soviet policy of "peaceful coexistence" with the West that Mao sought to undermine.[61] Mao believed that not only was this "coexistence" undesirable for his own personal political reasons, but he also believed that for some time the Soviet Union had looked down upon the Chinese, who they saw as second-rate and untrustworthy.[62] This sentiment was also echoed by the PRC's main diplomat, Zhou Enlai. In a 1957 report to Mao and the CCP central leadership, Zhou made it clear that he viewed the Soviets as self-centered allies: "In my view, the mistakes of the Soviet communist leadership arise from erroneous thinking. They often set the interests of the Soviet Communist Party ahead of their brotherly parties; they often set their own interests as the leaders ahead of those of the party. As a result, they often fail to overcome subjectivity, narrow-mindedness, and emotion."[63] By pursuing peaceful coexistence with the West, the Soviet Union was overlooking the concerns of its ally and forcing China into a junior-partner role in international geopolitics.

Mao's distaste for peaceful coexistence also stemmed from his, and by proxy the CCP's, approach to Marxist-Leninist thought. For Mao and those around him, it was clear that as Marx had predicted, the capitalist world (i.e. the United States) would eventually and dramatically fall, thus leaving the proletarian masses victorious. Pursuing such a rapprochement with the United States in 1959–60 was anathema, in Mao's mind, to proletarian revolution and the fight against capitalist imperialism.[64]

In February 1960, a Chinese delegation was invited to a Warsaw Pact conference. Here, the Sino-Soviet rift was brought out into the open

From left to right: CPSU General Secretary Nikita Khrushchev, CCP Chairman Mao Zedong, President of North Vietnam Ho Chi Minh, and CCP Vice Chair Soong Ching-ling. Taken in 1959, relations between those present and their respective nations had already begun to fray. (Wikimedia Commons)

for the entirety of the communist world to see. During the conference, Mao's close advisor and de facto security chief Kang Sheng accused Khruschev of "revising, emasculating, and betraying" the legacy of Lenin. Khruschev retorted, "I am General Secretary of the Communist Party of the Soviet Union ... your credentials are much more shallow than mine!" As the exchange became more heated, one of the Soviet participants noticed the rage in Kang's eyes: "You could see at first glance, he was a very evil and ruthless person."[65] These bitter exchanges, while kept under wraps in Moscow, were published in full in various Beijing media outlets. A month after the conference, the Soviets pulled their scientific and technological advisors from the PRC.[66]

Peaceful coexistence with the West became a continued priority for the final years of Khrushchev's tenure. The contentious Cuban Missile Crisis of October 1962, while harrowing, opened the door to continued dialogue between the U.S. and Soviet Union regarding nuclear weapons. That December, Khrushchev expressed these hopes to visiting Yugoslav leader Josef Broz Tito. During the conversation, Khrushchev referred to Mao and the PRC as "dogmatists" who sought to push the communist camp towards another world war.[67] Forging ahead with nuclear talks with the United States, Khrushchev agreed to a Limited Test Ban Treaty with the United States and the United Kingdom on August 5, 1963.

Over 80 nations would agree to the treaty in the next month alone, but the PRC stood fast in its condemnation of the treaty. In a discussion with Kenyan political leaders a month to the day after the signing of the treaty, Zhou Enlai proclaimed, "We will not fall for Western tricks, and will not be manipulated. We have come to a conclusion. The Three-Nation Treaty is a huge swindle."[68] According to historian Lorenz Lüthi, the disagreements thus far between the CPSU and CCP had placed their relationship on a knife-edge. The Limited Test Ban Treaty "burst into the open" the final split between the two parties.[69] The following year, the PRC published the infamous "nine polemics" which denounced the Soviet Union and Khrushchev's policies in their entirety. One such polemic issued on February 3, 1963, entitled "The Leaders of the CPSU Are the Greatest Splitters of Our Times," clearly labels the Soviets as a threat to socialist unity, and states that a split from Soviet policy was the only way to save the socialist camp from complete ruin.[70]

In July 1963, a Chinese delegation traveled to Moscow at the Soviets' behest in a last-ditch effort to maintain internationalist solidarity within the communist camp. However, the Chinese had already made up their minds. Just prior to the talks, Zhou Enlai exclaimed, "These talks may in fact go two ways: one is delay, one is split."[71] Between July 5 and July 20, 1963, Soviet and Chinese interlocutors engaged in long-winded accusations and counter-accusations against one another. To the Chinese, the Soviets had capitulated in Cuba during the 1962 missile crisis, engaged in "great power chauvinism," and had tried to "bind China by hand and feet." These were but a few of the litany of accusations leveled by the PRC delegation.[72] Kang Sheng, once again holding nothing back, launched into a piercing polemic denouncing Khruschev and de-Stalinization:

> Can it really be that the CPSU, which for a long time had the love and respect of the revolutionary peoples of the whole world, had a "bandit" as its great leader for several decades? From what you have said it appears as if the ranks of the international communist movement which grew and became stronger from year to year were under the leadership of some sort of "shit."

Kang continued, pointing out with "ferociously clenched teeth" that Khruschev was a hypocritical opportunist who had stood by Stalin during the Soviet Great Terror of the 1930s but now felt the need to denounce him.[73] Needless to say, the July talks concluded with zero trace of reconciliation between the two parties. In a very telling article from September 1963, Chinese state media made sure to lay the entirety of the blame at Khrushchev's feet: "Not all the water in the Volga [River] can wash away the great shame you have brought upon the CPSU and upon the Soviet Union."[74] Thus the die had been cast for the DRV. North Vietnamese leaders now needed to navigate the worsening divorce of its two largest patrons at a time when events in Vietnam began to boil over.

North Vietnamese Political and Strategic Shifts and the Formation of PAVN's Armored Force (1956–63)

The end of the war against the French brought with it a new set of dilemmas for the fledgling Democratic Republic of Vietnam. Foremost of these was the issue of land reform. In an effort to reverse the practice of landlordism that had been established by the French, the North Vietnamese Politburo under the leadership of Truong Chinh began its land reform campaign in December 1953 in the hopes that it would place land into the hands of poor peasants and elevate the social status of North Vietnam's dispossessed. However, much like how the PRC's Great Leap Forward progressed, the land reform in North Vietnam quickly floundered, with severe consequences for Hanoi.

Hanoi's attempt at land reform, while nominally an effort to reduce poverty, was largely to exert control over North Vietnam's populace down to the village level and "purify the [Vietnamese Workers' Party] of bourgeois or capitalist elements who had been tolerated during the exigencies of the French War."[75] Land reform quickly devolved into brutal and sadistic excesses that shocked even the Politburo in Hanoi. "Old" party members were often killed outright via public lynchings and firing squads. Villagers turned against their neighbors and began a tit-for-tat series of retaliations. In some instances, supposed bourgeois collaborators had excrement forced into their mouths as a form of public humiliation.

By 1956, the land reform situation had gotten so heinous that it received public rebuke from Hanoi. On December 1, 1956, Nguyen Van Hong, the vice minister of justice, decried the excesses of what was supposed to be a strengthening of North Vietnamese societal cohesion: "In some areas, there is no regard for the law, while in others it is openly flouted. This grave situation is greatly damaging the moral and material life of the population as well as the prestige of the government."[76]

Two major shifts occurred as a result of the land reform fiasco. First, the prestige of Ho Chi Minh and his top allies, namely Pham Van Dong and Truong Chinh, was severely tainted. Truong Chinh, while not completely ousted from the Politburo, was forced to step down as first secretary. This led to a reform campaign called the "rectification of errors" aimed at righting the wrongs of the land reform scheme. The rectification of errors, while seeking to cool political temperatures in North Vietnam, led to a new round of party purges. These purges eliminated the political rivals of two Politburo members who, by 1960, would be the most prominent political voices in North Vietnam: Le Duc Tho and Le Duan. Capitalizing off the havoc wrought by land reform and internecine party politics, Le Duan and Le Duc Tho ascended to the centers of power within the Politburo. As the years progressed, their power only increased, and by 1964 it had become nearly complete.[77]

The second byproduct of the tumultuous land reform years of 1954–56 was the opening of ideological and political rifts between Hanoi and Beijing. As previously discussed, Beijing had been the foremost patron and supporter of Ho Chi Minh's independence effort during the First Indochina War. Many of the military tactics and strategy (as well as political philosophy) adopted by the DRV had their origins in the PRC. The land reform efforts of 1954–56 also had their origins in Chinese political thought. As historian Qiang Zhai explains, "The destruction and instability generated by the land reform indicated the folly of introducing the drastic Maoist formula of class struggle in a small and fragile rural society where many landlords and rich peasants had identified with the Communist Party in opposing France."[78] With the failure of Maoist collectivization approaches still haunting sectors of the Politburo in 1956, Hanoi began to move away from the PRC model of class struggle, mass mobilization, and continuous revolution, and instead began to adopt a Soviet model of "centralization and managerial control."[79]

The disastrous conclusion of the DRV's land reform and the widening Sino-Soviet split came at a time when events both north and south of the 17th Parallel had reached a breaking point. As per the Geneva Agreement, July 1956 marked the mandated timeframe in which elections on both sides of the 17th Parallel would determine the fate and proposed reunification of Vietnam. However, the RVN government of President Ngo Dinh Diem rebuffed calls for elections. Despite pleading from the DRV to apply international pressure on Diem and enforce the tenets of the Geneva Accords, by early 1957 the international community (including the PRC and Soviet Union) had begun to accept what was once a temporary partition as a more permanent one.[80]

Recently empowered and more aggressive personalities such as that of Le Duan began to push for a more belligerent approach to unifying Vietnam. Le Duan in 1956 published an essay that was read and approved by the Eleventh Plenum[†] which called for increased "political struggle" in the South while simultaneously tabling the option for an armed struggle if the provisions of the Geneva Agreement were not adhered to. Three years later, as the Diem regime solidified its power, it continued to ignore the Geneva Agreement and began to target its political opponents. Hanoi under the direction of Le Duan decided to shift its strategy dramatically and suddenly. The Fifteenth Plenum of May 1959 not only solidified Le Duan as the effective leader of DRV strategy going forward, but it set the stage for the American War in Vietnam. The Fifteenth Plenum shifted away from political struggle and formally embraced the strategy of armed struggle and liberation in the South. Specifically, the war for Southern liberation would take the form of a Vietnamized version of Mao's people's war strategy.[81]

[†] For a more detailed description of Vietnamese Workers' Party terms, see the introductory chapter of Pierre Asselin's *Vietnam's American War*. A plenum is a meeting of the Central Committee of the VWP Politburo during a given Congressional period. The Eleventh Plenum therefore was the 11th time the Central Committee had met during the 1951 VWP Congress. Subsequent VWP Congressional Sessions in 1960 and 1976 restarted the count of plenum meetings.

The strategy of "people's war" stemmed from the experiences of Mao's communist forces during the Chinese Civil War. Following a concept of "three-stage" warfare, a people's war involved periods of retrenchment and protracted warfare, building popular support (especially amongst the peasantry), and eventually engaging in an all-out assault on the enemy's urban centers.[82] However, a strict people's war approach would not work in Vietnam. While adopted at the outset of Ho Chi Minh's war against the French, a strict adherence to the people's war model was found to be wanting and an absolute decisive victory over the French was deemed unlikely.

Dien Bien Phu, while decisive, did not in "one fell swoop" defeat the entirety of French forces in Indochina. With the advent of a divided Vietnam following Geneva, the promotion of a "by the book" people's war seemed to be even further from reality. This was largely due to the fact that with the Geneva Accords in place, reunification could be achieved through national elections. However, once this optimistic projection proved to be naïve and the Fifteenth Plenum's declaration took hold, there was once again a renewed debate over whether a people's war approach would work. Le Duan pushed back against a flat-out adoption of the Chinese model but instead pushed for a hybrid approach that adhered to the unique situations within South Vietnam.

In 1960, the creation of the National Liberation Front of South Vietnam (or "Viet Cong" as it was referred to by South Vietnamese and later, American observers) sought to solidify the political consciousness of the South Vietnamese peasantry, while the Politburo simultaneously called for an intensification of the military effort with the ultimate goal of a combined General Offensive and Uprising prescribed for the eventual liberation of the South. However, the newly inaugurated general secretary of the Third Party Congress, Le Duan, urged caution. While it was decided that tenets of the people's war approach (such as the politicization of the South Vietnamese peasantry) should continue, Le Duan argued that a rush to emphasize military force might provoke the United States into open conflict at a time when the revolution in the South was still in its "first stage of development." This caution continued into 1963. Once again, fears that increased DRV military pressure on the South would invoke the wrath of the United States overrode the strategic opportunity that had arisen with the continued political upheaval in Saigon.[83]

While DRV strategists debated the best course of action vis-à-vis South Vietnam, Sino-Soviet disputes continued unabated. The VWP's Third Congress convened in September 1960, with both Soviet and PRC representatives present. At the meeting, Le Duan stated that the struggle in the South would be "long and arduous ... not simple but complex, combining many forms of struggle."[84] Thus, Le Duan sought to strike a compromise between the overtly aggressive people's war model of the PRC and the current Soviet diplomatic strategy of peaceful coexistence.

While out of power but nonetheless an important international figurehead and rallying point, Ho Chi Minh continued to try to patch together Sino-Soviet relations. At the Moscow Conference of November 1960, Ho attempted to help bridge the gap between the two parties, but to little avail. Though he'd told Soviet leader Nikita Khruschev that the PRC needed to be kept within the socialist camp, Ho failed in his mission to achieve communist solidarity. Despite a statement on March 10, 1962, declaring an expansion in Sino-Vietnamese and Soviet-Vietnamese friendship associations in the DRV, Hanoi had failed to help bridge the gap between Beijing and Moscow.

In a rather innocuous visit to Beijing in October 1961 as part of a state dinner visit, Deputy Minister of Culture of North Vietnam Lê Kiêm (who had just visited Moscow) summed up Hanoi's predicament rather well in a conversation with his PRC counterparts: "because both the Chinese Communist Party and the Soviet Communist Party are large parties, we Vietnamese were left in a difficult situation when the two large parties had different views."[85] Thus was the situation between Hanoi and its benefactors in Beijing and Moscow; a struggling ally found itself trying to bind together an already fractured and animosity-filled relationship.

While DRV politicians continued to debate strategy and the proper navigation of an increasingly divided communist world, the People's Liberation Armed Forces of Vietnam (PLAF) began to modernize. As VWP plenums called for an increased struggle in the South, the PLAF began to create specialty branches within each of its armed forces. One such specialty branch was a modernized armored force. According to the official history of PAVN's armor branch, two groups of PAVN officers and enlisted men were selected to be sent abroad for armored training. The first group, consisting of 54 personnel, were trained on commanding tanks, tank techniques, and armored technology. The second group, consisting of 147 personnel, were given extensive training on the various roles and duties within a tank. Upon the completion of their training, these two groups were formally christened as the 202nd Tank Regiment by the North Vietnamese Ministry of Defense on October 5, 1959. The 202nd was comprised of "three tank combat battalions, one maintenance and repair company, one engineer company, one security company, one training company, one signal/communications company, and four headquarters staff agencies: Operations Staff, Political, Rear Services, and Technical."[86]

One year after the formation of the 202nd, in July 1960, the newly formed tank regiment received its first shipment of Soviet tanks at the Vinh Yen train station north of Hanoi. However, these tanks were semi-dated (for 1960) T-34s. While the T-34 served valiantly with the Soviet Army during World War II, it had long been eclipsed by more modern tanks such as the Soviet T-54 and the American M48 Patton. Nonetheless, the 202nd engaged in four separate exercises between 1960–61. One such exercise conducted alongside an infantry regiment from PAVN's 308th Division saw the 202nd practice maneuvering tanks through difficult, wet terrain. In a later exercise, the 202nd also performed live-fire training at a training center north of Phuc Yen. In perhaps the most fascinating training exercise undertaken by PAVN's nascent armor corps, the 202nd practiced assaulting enemy positions during a simulated detonation of a nuclear weapon in December 1961.[87]

Several months prior to its nuclear training, the 202nd received an upgrade with regards to its inventory. A new tank battalion was added to the regiment, as well as more modern Soviet-built T-54s and PT-76s (an amphibious tank adept at traversing Vietnam's rivers and rice paddies). In addition to new tanks, the 202nd was also reorganized to encompass several combat support companies dealing with maintenance, antiaircraft defense, engineering, and communications.[88] While it took seven more years for PAVN armor to appear on the battlefields of South Vietnam, the formation of the 202nd in 1959 illustrates that PAVN (and by proxy the VWP Politburo) anticipated an intensification of military action in the South.

The First Indochina War helped establish the relationship between the newly declared Democratic Republic of Vietnam and its allies in Beijing and Moscow. When comparing the DRV's two patrons during this period, it is clear that the PRC played a larger role in arming, advising, and aiding the political and military forces of Ho Chi Minh than the Soviet Union. Events in Europe (and later the calls for peaceful coexistence with the West) were a larger priority for Josef Stalin and his successor, Nikita Khrushchev. While Moscow encouraged and publicly supported the DRV, Hanoi was never a focal point for Soviet policymakers from 1954–63. The PRC, however, viewed Vietnam as one of its utmost geostrategic interests and sought to build up Hanoi as an effective buffer against Western powers. The "betrayal" at Geneva opened the first cracks in the Sino-Soviet-Vietnamese relationship. Moscow and Beijing's fear of American intervention, as well as a general desire to bring an end to hostilities regardless of compromise, overrode the wishes of the VWP to bring Vietnam under complete communist control. The sense of betrayal only worsened as the RVN government negated the terms of Geneva in 1956 and the PRC and Soviet Union stood idly by. Going forward, the DRV realized that neither Moscow or Beijing could consistently be counted on as steadfast, unwavering allies.

To make matters worse, the DRV had to navigate incredibly precarious geopolitical waters as the Soviets and Chinese began to openly divorce themselves from one another. Questions of VWP strategy, as well as diplomacy, were placed within the context of a worsening trilateral relationship. Moscow and Beijing, in subsequent years, used Vietnam as a means of jockeying for the title of leader of the communist world. Hanoi, which could ill afford to alienate either the PRC or the Soviet Union, was henceforth driven to play both sides in a delicate balancing act.

Early attempts by Hanoi to build a prosperous communist state in line with Maoist principles floundered dramatically. This paved the way for a new generation of VWP leaders, such as Le Duan, advocating a more aggressive stance vis-à-vis the Southern half of Vietnam. With this aggression came the modernization of PAVN's training and equipment. The advent of an armored force in 1959, several months after the dramatic declarations of the VWP's Fifteenth Plenum, was no coincidence. Hanoi was preparing for an increased struggle in the South, and the creation of a modernized armored force was a key part of this preparation. The fight for South Vietnam, as well as Sino-Soviet intrigue with regards to Vietnam, shifted dramatically when the USS *Maddox* and USS *Turner Joy* entered the Gulf of Tonkin in the summer of 1964.

CHAPTER 2

Evolving Alliances and Shifting Strategies (1964–71)

1964: The Gulf of Tonkin and Sino-Soviet-Vietnamese Attitudinal Shifts

The end of 1963 brought about drastic changes not only to DRV strategy, but to Hanoi's relationships with Beijing and Moscow. On November 1, a dramatic coup in South Vietnam by segments of the South Vietnamese military was launched against RVN President Ngo Dinh Diem. Largely in response to Diem's harsh crackdown towards the South Vietnamese Buddhist community in the previous months, the coup was launched with tacit American approval. After two days of chaotic street fighting between pro- and anti-presidential forces, Diem—alongside his brother and political confidant, Ngo Dinh Nhu—was escorted out of a Catholic church in the Cholon neighborhood of Saigon and into an M-113 armored personnel carrier by forces loyal to the coup plotters. The brothers were assured by their captors that they would not be harmed. As Diem and his brother were driven through Saigon, the M-113 made a sudden stop at a railroad crossing. As the creaking of the gears subsided, the roar of a sub-machine gun filled the interior of the armored vehicle. Diem and his brother were executed in a hail of gunfire that would have profound consequences for both sides of the 17th Parallel.[1]

A military junta under the leadership of Army of ARVN General Duong Van Minh took control of South Vietnam after Diem's ouster. Renewed debate in Hanoi erupted as Saigon still smoldered. In 1960, a new VWP congress commenced. By December 1963 it had reached its 9th Plenum. The 9th Plenum was called to address the drastically changing and evolving events happening south of the 17th parallel. Several courses of action, as well as their advocates within the Politburo, began to emerge during the December 1964 meeting. Option one called for a wait-and-see approach: hold back and observe the still-chaotic events in Saigon. Option two proposed extending an olive branch to the new junta in Saigon and seeing if General Minh would be open to peace talks. Option three, a sort of "nuclear" option, suggested a large-scale invasion of the South aimed at knocking out General Minh's government before it could get proper footing. The first two of these options were adopted by Ho Chi Minh and his fellow "doves" within the Politburo. The final, most drastic option was vehemently pursued and advocated for by none other than the firebrand of 1959's Fifteenth Plenum, Le Duan.[2]

Le Duan, whose power had been bolstered by Ho's disastrous land reform as well as the events of previous plenums, came into the 9th Plenum with a decidedly hawkish attitude. Le Duan diplomatically yet sternly castigated the doves within the audience for believing that the situation in the South could be corrected via peaceful or nonaggressive means. According to Le Duan, a failure to capitalize on the chaotic situation south of the 17th Parallel would do nothing but harm Hanoi's revolutionary struggle in the long run. PAVN General Vo Nguyen Giap, the hero of Dien Bien Phu, warned Le Duan that a premature offensive against the Saigon government could spell serious problems for the then-undermanned and undertrained North Vietnamese Army. However, Le Duan and his fellow hawks won the day and authored a new, even more aggressive strategy for the war for Southern liberation, entitled "Resolution 9."[3]

The strategy of Resolution 9 called for a "General Offensive and General Uprising" that would, in the estimation of Le Duan and his fellow hawks, secure victory for the DRV in 1964. The General Offensive and General Uprising strategy was a rehashing of the Maoist concept of people's war. The people's war model maintained a three-step process that needed to be followed for ultimate victory: defense/guerilla war, equilibrium/parity with enemy forces, and ultimately a general counteroffensive leading to victory.[4] The Maoist model called for protracted warfare with an utmost emphasis on caution. In Mao's own words, "We must not attack objectives we are not certain of winning. We must confine our operations to relatively small areas and destroy the enemy and traitors in those places."[5]

While borrowing some aspects of the people's war concept, such as the general counteroffensive, Le Duan's Resolution 9 adopted a go-for-broke strategy (bypassing the protracted-struggle phase) which called for a major buildup of PAVN forces in the Central Highlands of South Vietnam. Resolution 9 was adopted by the attendees of the 9th Plenum, but not without great consternation and debate. The debate surrounding Resolution 9 had to deal not only with concerns over unpreparedness, but also concerns surrounding the widening Sino-Soviet split. By pursuing such an aggressive stance towards the South, the DRV was, in essence, formally eschewing the Soviet policy of "peaceful coexistence" and embracing the more aggressive stance of the PRC.[6]

Mao Zedong (left) and Vietnamese Workers' Party General Secretary Le Duan (right) share a toast in August 1964. By the end of the decade, their relationship had gone from friendly to antagonistic. (Wikimedia Commons)

A report from the United States Military Assistance Command, Vietnam (MACV) stated that the resolution "contained an in-depth treatment of the Sino-Soviet ideological split." However, while trying to "walk a middle line," Resolution 9 "carefully defined a position more in agreement with Communist China."[7] Moderate plenum attendees argued with Le Duan and his coterie of hawks that not only was the VWP drastically reneging on its own previous stances, but it was on course to terminate the good will extended at the Moscow Conference of 1960.

While not overtly excoriating the USSR and the CPSU, Resolution 9 and Le Duan did almost everything short of that.[8] Internally however, Le Duan and his allies began to openly persecute and alienate those who were deemed in lockstep with Moscow's line. In what was later called the Revisionist Anti-Party Affair, Le Duan and his band of triumphant hawks sought to quell the remaining pockets of dissent.[9] On March 10, 1964, the purges of the VWP began. With fears of a looming American intervention in Vietnam used as a pretext, Le Duan ordered a "militarization of the whole country" as well as mandatory "re-education" for all party members. The purges the DRV underwent at this time, noted one observer, were "reminiscent of the reign of terror during the agricultural reforms of 1953–55 in the Soviet Union or in the last days of the Stalin regime, containing all the elements of an explosive internal or external eruption."[10]

Vocal moderates who had held significant positions of power in the VWP were ousted from their seats in the Politburo. Even North Vietnamese students who had been sent abroad to Eastern Europe and the USSR were called back to the DRV to receive reeducation, starting in early 1964.[11] Perhaps the greatest effect this new round of purges had was the de facto defenestration of two of the VWP Politburo's most notable and distinguished members, Ho Chi Minh and Vo Nguyen Giap. While both men retained their positions within the Politburo, their powers were reduced to that of mere figureheads. The doves that remained within the VWP were pressured into silence and in some cases even retired. As historian Pierre Asselin notes "Soon, an unprecedented air of repressiveness descended upon Hanoi and the rest of the North. Those bold or foolish enough to speak against the regime ... had to answer to the Ministry of Public Security."[12]

Le Duan's performance at the 9th Plenum of the VWP's 1960 congress was nothing short of masterful. His political maneuvering managed to not only solidify his power amongst the party, but it also set Hanoi on a path to war. Resolution 9 called for a much more aggressive strategy aimed at South Vietnam which simultaneously placed Hanoi in the PRC camp and at odds with the Soviet Union. However, major events in the late summer and early fall of 1964 again shifted the dynamics of not just North Vietnamese strategy, but the geopolitical dispositions of its two biggest patrons.

At 1540 Saigon time on August 2, 1964, Commander of the U.S. Pacific Fleet Admiral Ulysses Sharp cabled the Joint Chiefs of Staff in Washington, DC. The USS *Maddox* had been engaged by North Vietnamese torpedo boats in the Gulf of Tonkin directly off the coast of North Vietnam. Two of the vessels that engaged the *Maddox* were struck by gunfire, as well as strafing aircraft from the USS *Ticonderoga* damaging them, while a third vessel was left dead in the water. Two days later at 0900 hours Washington time, the USS *Maddox* and USS *Turner Joy* reported another attack from hostile torpedo boats. While reports about a second attack remained unverified at best, plans within the White House began to immediately take shape regarding a retaliatory response.

Secretary of Defense Robert McNamara met with the National Security Council and U.S. congressional leaders at 1815 to discuss the day's events, present "evidence" of the attacks, and foment a plan for military retaliation.[13] At 2336 that evening, President Lyndon Johnson declared in a televised White House address that "aggression by terror against the peaceful villagers of South Viet-Nam [*sic*] has now been joined by open aggression on the high seas against the United States of America." Johnson went on to say, "we still seek no wider war" and "firmness in the right is indispensable today for peace." One hour and thirty minutes after the address, U.S. Navy fighter bombers began the first of 62 sorties aimed at destroying North Vietnamese naval vessels and oil facilities in and around the port city of Vinh.[14] In the previous day's meeting with the National Security Council, CIA Director John A. McCone espoused feelings of optimism: "The proposed U.S. reprisals will result in a sharp North Vietnamese military reaction, but such actions would not represent a deliberate decision to provoke or accept a major escalation of the Vietnamese war."[15] McCone's prediction, however, proved to be fatally flawed.

The Gulf of Tonkin incident, as history would remember the events of August 2 and 4, 1964, changed the course of the Vietnam War and, by proxy, North Vietnam's disposition towards Beijing and Moscow. Immediately following the events of early August, the United States adopted the Gulf of Tonkin Resolution which, in essence, was an American version of Resolution 9. The Gulf of Tonkin Resolution gave incredibly broad powers to the Johnson administration with regards to utilizing military force in Southeast Asia.[16] President Johnson's desire to appear hawkish during a presidential campaign year, as well as a sitting U.S. Congress that wished to demonstrate "solidarity behind both the reprisal and [Johnson's] Vietnam policy in general," led to the overwhelming passage of the resolution, firmly solidifying America's path to direct intervention in Southeast Asia.[17]

Reactions to the Gulf of Tonkin incident and subsequent congressional resolution in the communist world were also dramatic in their effect on the war in Vietnam. The PRC reacted quickly to the events of August 4, 1964 by sending a cable to Hanoi the following day advising the North Vietnamese to "investigate and clarify the situation, discuss and formulate proper strategies and policies, and be ready to take action."[18] In a meeting on August 6 with the Algerian ambassador to the PRC, Zhou Enlai expressed great concern that the Gulf of Tonkin was in fact a "probing" mission aimed at provoking the North Vietnamese.

U.S. President Lyndon Johnson addresses the American public after the Gulf of Tonkin incident, August 1964. (Wikimedia Commons/LBJ Presidential Library)

Zhou Enlai emphatically went on to declare the PRC's continued support for the DRV: "America will test the Vietnamese resolve to resist. Once tested, Vietnam will certainly resist. Actually, America already knows they will resist, and once they do test they will be even surer that if they set the flames of war, the fire will be inextinguishable. China will definitely stand by Vietnam. That is for certain."[19]

Mao began to utilize the events of August 1964 to once again organize and mobilize the Chinese populace. This new political mobilization, the Resist America and Assist Vietnam Movement, saw 20 million Chinese citizens take to the streets in the week following the Gulf of Tonkin incident to protest what was seen as naked American imperialist aggression.[20] Between August and September 1964, the PRC began to move air defense units as well as fighter aircraft to its Sino-Vietnamese border provinces. Additionally, Chinese Army observers were sent to North Vietnam to assess the situation in the event that Beijing decided to deploy troops in support of Hanoi. On October 5, Mao told a North Vietnamese delegation in Beijing to be wary of a direct American invasion.[21]

While the PRC continued its role as the more aggressive, fire-breathing patron of the DRV, the Soviet Union underwent a major shift in its disposition towards the war in Southeast Asia. The events on the high seas in August 1964 were met with profound shock within the party confines of the CPSU. News of the incident was covered in the state newspaper *Pravda* on August 3, with the majority of its readers unsure of where the Gulf of Tonkin was. Regardless, this watershed moment off the coast of Vietnam forced the Soviet Union to confront its Vietnam policy in stark terms: to escalate or to not escalate? On August 5, Soviet news agency TASS issued a proclamation aimed at the United States warning against escalation of the conflict.[22] That same day, Soviet leader Nikita Khrushchev wrote a letter to President Johnson pleading for a de-escalation of hostilities. With his guiding principle of peaceful coexistence, as well as the recent memory of the Cuban Missile crisis, Khrushchev pleaded:

> It would be unnecessary to speak in detail now about the enormous responsibility which our two powers bear, you personally as President of the United States

and I as Chairman of the U.S.S.R. Council of Ministers, in keeping the peace, in ensuring that dangerous events whichever area of the globe they begin with, would not become first elements in the chain of ever more critical and maybe irreversible events.[23]

Two days later, President Johnson responded with a letter of his own. Johnson, while echoing his Soviet counterparts mentioning "heavy responsibility," stood firm in his support for the government of South Vietnam and the protection of U.S. military personnel in the region. Additionally, Johnson implored Khrushchev to "restrain either the North Vietnamese or [Beijing] from further reckless action."[24] Despite this back and forth, Khrushchev did not change his tune nor his country's stance on Vietnam. During the Khrushchev era, the policy of peaceful coexistence and a Eurocentric worldview made the conflict in Vietnam, at best, a secondary priority for Soviet policymakers. In the days following the Gulf of Tonkin, the Soviet Union joined the United States in calls for the United Nations to resolve the Vietnam issue. On August 10, 1965, Le Duan voiced his frustrations with what he saw as Soviet manipulation to Mao: "the Soviet revisionists want to use us as a bargaining chip."[25] The continued cold shoulder emanating from Moscow was largely because Soviet policymakers continued to view North Vietnam as a potential losing horse. Soviet diplomats in Hanoi believed that PAVN as well as the Viet Cong were overconfident and overzealous. Additionally, the Soviets were dismissive of the support that the DRV had received from the PRC thus far, referring to the support as merely "noise."[26]

However, Moscow's disposition towards Vietnam dramatically changed as the CPSU underwent a decisive overhaul in October of 1964. Nikita Khrushchev by this time had overstayed his welcome as leader of the Soviet Union. Members of the CPSU Politburo viewed him as "uncollegial [sic] and rash," and claimed that he denigrated his fellow colleagues while often acting unilaterally. With his back against the wall, Khrushchev simply told his comrades, "I thank you for the opportunity you have given me to retire."[27] A desire for a more "collectivist" leadership led the CPSU Politburo to select Khrushchev's own protégé as successor, Leonid Brezhnev. Brezhnev, who had risen to the top of CPSU leadership in 1956, wanted to repair what he and others within the Politburo viewed as a weakening of Soviet prestige.[28] While primarily caused by domestic factors, Khrushchev's ouster was also caused by his foreign policy. However, the Soviet Union's Vietnam policy was not an immediate concern.[29] This very fact is highlighted in the famous Polyansky Report which was issued throughout the CPSU following Khrushchev's dismissal. The report, which chronicled and criticized Khrushchev's foreign policy vis-à-vis Cuba and Latin America, did not mention Southeast Asia once, let alone Vietnam.[30]

Brezhnev's ascension, however, did coincide with a shift in Soviet foreign policy towards Vietnam. CPSU Politburo members Sergei Trapeznikov, V. A. Golikov, and V. I. Stepakov were (in addition to being close confidants of Brezhnev) instrumental in helping shape this new foreign policy. Unlike Khrushchev, these three individuals eschewed any suggestion of peaceful coexistence with the United States. Reflecting this newfound consensus, Golikov emphatically said during Politburo discussions, "We must not forget that world war is coming."[31] As the war in Vietnam continued to escalate during the fall of 1964, Brezhnev began to reach out to the DRV while simultaneously rebuffing American efforts at rekindling nuclear arms negotiations.

Being receptive to this newfound attention, Hanoi again began to carefully navigate the diplomatic waters between both Moscow and Beijing. Despite initial coolness between DRV and Soviet officials, Le Duan and the VWP sought to establish a new and hopefully fruitful relationship with the new leadership in Moscow. For example, in late November 1964 at the November Solidarity Conference for Vietnam in Hanoi, DRV officials refrained from open criticism of the Soviet Union and persistently implored their Chinese counterparts to refrain from needless invectives aimed at Moscow. The Chinese delegation, angered at the fact that they could not utilize the conference for anti-Soviet grandstanding, reportedly "left Hanoi by plane not very happy."[32]

While the DRV began to explore ways in which it could mend its relations with the Soviet Union, the Soviets tried to repair their frayed relationship with the PRC. The escalating war in Vietnam in the fall of 1964 appeared to be an opportunity for Soviet leadership to mend their relationship with Beijing. The trio of foreign policy advisors surrounding

Brezhnev, Golikov, Stepakov, and Trapeznikov had an affinity for the PRC's dogmatic approach to foreign policy. Accordingly, they among others argued for a renewed pro-China foreign policy that would use the "fraternal duty" of support for the DRV to hopefully reconcile the toxic relationship that existed between Beijing and Moscow.[33] However, a rather comedic diplomatic episode in November 1964 negated any small sense of progress being made between the Soviet Union and the PRC.

On November 7, 1964, delegates from across the communist world gathered in Moscow to celebrate the 47th anniversary of the October Revolution that brought about the founding of the Soviet Union. Foremost among the attendees was PRC delegate and Prime Minister Zhou Enlai. Despite a rousing speech from Brezhnev calling for a "new international meeting of the fraternal parties," Zhou remained reserved and detached during the evening's events.[34] Immediately following Brezhnev's speech was an awkward gaffe that solidified the mutual distrust between Beijing and Moscow. In what was meant to be an informal cocktail party for attendees later that evening, an offhand comment severed any chance of Sino–Soviet rapprochement. Visibly drunk, the Soviet Minister of Defense Rodion Malinovskii stumbled up to members of the PRC delegation and declared "I do not want any Mao and Khrushchev to hamper us…. We already did away with Khrushchev, now you should do away with Mao."[35] Present at this exchange was Zhou Enlai, who immediately left the banquet "red-faced."[36]

The subsequent Soviet reaction to Malinovskii's loose-lipped polemic did not help. During a meeting of party functionaries later that month, Brezhnev lambasted him for his "inconsiderable statement" and for "lack of tact," but there was no public denunciation of Malinovskii, nor was he removed from his ministerial post. To the Chinese, this lack of punishment was perceived as a tacit approval of Malinovskii's statements.[37]

While Sino-Soviet relations were arguably in an irreconcilable position prior to Malinovskii's comments, this awkward exchange prevented any sort of repair. Additionally, due to Mao's personality cult, these drunken comments led to a massive overreaction on the part of the Chinese. On November 21, the CCP began to once again publish open denunciations of the "modern revisionists" who infested the CPSU.[38] This type of denunciation was met in kind by the Soviets, who now eschewed the idea that the rising specter of large-scale conflict in Vietnam could be used as a conciliatory issue aimed at bridging the gap between Moscow and Beijing.

In December of 1964, the Soviet Union's ambassador to North Vietnam, Ilia Shcherbakov, met with his East German counterpart, Wolfgang Bertold, regarding recent events. Shcherbakov expressed satisfaction that Soviet-Vietnamese relations had progressed in a very positive light since Khrushchev's ouster in October. However, Shcherbakov expressed concern that "the Chinese only use the Vietnamese as a tool for their own, Chinese policy. Such doubts have emerged, among other issues, as the consequence of the events in August and of the related, insufficient aid from the People's Republic of China." Shcherbakov went on to express that the PRC seemed to be using the armed forces of North Vietnam to its own advantage.[39] The events of 1964 set in motion a tectonic shift in relations between Hanoi, Moscow, and Beijing. This year marked not only a shift in Soviet political and diplomatic postures, but it also represented the high-water mark for the PRC's influence in the global communist movement, as well as national liberation movements.[40] Subsequent years redefined and solidified these relationships in ways that would profoundly shape the course of North Vietnam's quest for victory.

The Cultural Revolution, the Rise of Soviet-Vietnamese Cooperation, and the Countdown to Tet (1965–67)

After the tumultuous events of the previous year, 1965 became the year of escalation for the war in Vietnam. The first PAVN units had begun to make their way south during the closing months of 1964 amid U.S. escalation. By early 1965, these units had reached their staging areas along the Cambodian border and in the Central Highlands in preparation for the upcoming winter–spring campaign. While the results of this early PAVN offensive were mixed at best, it helped cause yet another major escalation in the Vietnam War.

In March of 1965, in response to heightened North Vietnamese offensive action in the South, the United States deployed the first of hundreds and thousands of combat troops to South Vietnam. Hanoi once again amended its strategy for victory in light of the changing circumstances on the ground. The introduction of U.S. combat troops hindered Hanoi from implementing and successfully attaining the goals of Resolution 9 as quickly as was once thought possible. Instead, PAVN in conjunction with the VC would try to militarily destroy the ARVN while simultaneously inflicting casualties on U.S. forces.

The strategy of attrition called for quick, decisive engagements with U.S. forces. These engagements, while not aimed at completely destroying U.S. units, sought to damage enemy units while protecting PAVN/VC forces in the hopes that the enemy would eventually be worn down. Simultaneously, Hanoi launched a two-pronged political offensive within the confines of Vietnam as well as abroad. Within Vietnam, Hanoi sought to mobilize its own populace as well as vulnerable segments of the South Vietnamese populace. This included a strategy of undermining the morale of ARVN in the hopes that some ARVN troopers would desert and join the communist cause. The political struggle abroad sought to manipulate and shape world opinion to portray North Vietnam as a helpless, independence-minded nation forced to suffer the blows of a global superpower. "The Anti-American Resistance for National Salvation," as Hanoi called this strategy, needed amplification and distribution if it were to be successful.[41] However, the two biggest possible amplifiers of Hanoi's diplomatic struggle, the PRC and the Soviet Union, continued to divide the communist world.

A week before U.S. combat troops were deployed to Vietnam, PRC diplomatic superstar Zhou Enlai sat down with the aging and politically weakened Ho Chi Minh to express several concerns. Over the course of the conversation, Zhou warned Ho that the duplicity and chauvinist attitudes of the Soviet Union had not abated following the fall of Khrushchev. As their exchange continued, Zhou went so far as to accuse the Soviet Union of mishandling (either purposefully or otherwise) classified materials and intelligence: "So in our course of revolution, and in our struggle against the U.S., the matters of top secrecy should not be disclosed to them." Zhou went on to say that everything emanating from Moscow, from MiG fighter jets to weapons training, should be viewed with the utmost skepticism.[42] Highlighting the PRC's continued fear over heightened Soviet involvement in Vietnam, a cable from the Chinese embassy in Moscow dated April 10, 1965, entitled "Recent Responses from the Soviet Revisionists to the Situation in Vietnam," shows a sincere disdain for Brezhnev's newfound focus on Vietnam. The cable decried the Soviet Union's "phony call for solidarity against imperialism."[43]

Chinese concern over Soviet support for Vietnam continued well into 1965, especially when, in July 1965, the Soviets and North Vietnamese signed an agreement which boosted economic and military ties between the two countries. Largely in response to America's bombing of the North, as well as increased ground combat in the South, Hanoi happily accepted this increased Soviet aid for several key reasons. First, starting in 1965 the North Vietnamese were adopting a much more aggressive big-unit strategy in the South. The hybrid Vietnamese version of the Maoist people's war concept was beginning to become less and less applicable to the situation that PAVN and the VC found themselves in as America escalated its efforts in Vietnam. The types of dated and unreliable weaponry the PRC was still providing proved unsuitable for large-scale combat against the United States. This more aggressive kind of war necessitated heavy military technology which almost exclusively came from the Soviet Union.

The change in Soviet aid and arms was drastic. From 1960–64, Soviet economic aid to Vietnam was an estimated $400 million. From 1965–68, this aid increased to over $2.3 billion. In terms of military aid, Soviet arms shipments to Hanoi jumped from $125–90 million in 1960–64 to $1.4–.8 billion in 1965–68.[44] As historian Douglas Pike put it, "As 85 percent of the hardware being delivered [to North Vietnam] in the later years of the war was of the more sophisticated type, most came from the USSR and East Europe; China was simply unable to provide such aid."[45]

In light of this massive shift in Soviet support, the PRC doubled down on its warnings to Hanoi over what was seen as duplicitous maneuvering originating from Moscow. In a meeting with DRV Prime Minister Pham Van Dong in October 1965, Zhou Enlai ardently argued against Soviet aid to North Vietnam. In a tense rebuttal to Pham Van Dong, Zhou declared, "As you have asked for my opinion, I would like to tell you the following: I do not support the idea of Soviet volunteers going to Vietnam, nor [do I support] Soviet aid to Vietnam." Going further,

Zhou tried to assuage Pham Van Dong's fears regarding China's intent: "[As to] Vietnam, we always want to help. In our mind, our thoughts, we never think of selling out Vietnam. But we are always afraid of the revisionists standing between us."[46] These "revisionists" that Zhou warned of were the CPSU and its global representatives, which in the eyes of Mao and the PRC, were slowly becoming the greatest threat to not only the People's Republic, but to world communist revolutionaries. In order to reverse the tide of the revisionists, Mao Zedong launched a dramatic nationwide purge that became known as the Cultural Revolution.

The Cultural Revolution was, for all intents and purposes, the sequel to Mao's Great Leap Forward of the late 1950s. In the words of historian Frank Dikötter, "the Cultural Revolution was Mao's second attempt to become the historical pivot around which the socialist universe revolved."[47] Mao believed that the revisionism present in the Soviet Union both during and after the reign of Nikita Khrushchev was the result of unfinished revolutionary business. To Mao, while the Soviet Union's bourgeois was gone, bourgeois ideology maintained a firm grip on Soviet politics.[48]

Another reason Mao decided to launch the Cultural Revolution was due to the fallout of his disastrous Great Leap Forward. By the early 1960s, Mao was threatened with scathing criticism from within his own party. In 1962, during a meeting of top CCP leaders known as the Seven Thousand Cadres Conference, attendees railed against the failures of the Great Leap.[49] Sensing political danger, Mao formed the Cultural Revolution Group in the summer of 1964. The group gathered for the next two years and formulated plans to reassert Mao as the preeminent and unquestioned leader of the PRC.[50] Mao launched the Cultural Revolution in the summer of 1966 in large part, according to historian Sergey Radchenko "to create a China of Mao worshippers."[51]

As a means of wiping away the sins of the past, Mao leaned heavily into the student population of China to be the so called Red Guards of this new revolution.[52] The revolution of PRC culture was waged on an almost comedic level. Sofas were labeled as bourgeois. Revolutionaries debated whether city traffic lights should replace green with red as the symbol for "go." More alarmingly however were the forced confessions and torture of those deemed to represent the middle class and/or foreign influence. Some individuals accused of these heresies were executed in the street. It was commonplace for the executioners to send the families of the deceased a bill for the bullet that killed their loved one.[53]

In August of 1966, the Red Guards and a sea of 210,000 revolutionaries laid siege to the Soviet Embassy in Beijing. Soviet diplomats were prevented from leaving the compound, and East German diplomats traversing Beijing's streets were mistaken for Soviets and severely beaten. Much to the bafflement of Soviet officials, the Chinese did nothing to quell the violent mobs surrounding their embassy. In a response to an official Soviet communique denouncing the violence and breach of diplomatic protocol, the Chinese Foreign Ministry responded that "their [Red Guards and fellow protestors] actions correspond to the methods of the Cultural Revolution."[54] However, almost as quickly as it began, the Cultural Revolution descended into chaos.

The Red Guards, far from united, splintered into factionalized and regionalized fanatical mobs aimed at score settling and seizing power. By January 1967, the chaos of the revolution had become so great that the army was called in to quell the Red Guards.[55] However, Mao called in the army with orders to "support the left." With such vague instructions, open fighting began between factions of revolutionaries, with the Chinese Army caught in the middle. In Guangxi province, fighting (sometimes involving tens of thousands of people) in 1968 resulted in hundreds of fatalities.[56] In an announcement on July 3, 1968, Mao called for a cessation of violence across the nation. By September, Zhou Enlai announced that the revolution had been victorious.[57] However, the damage—both domestic and international—had already been done.

The Cultural Revolution further strained Hanoi's weakening relationship with Beijing. First and foremost, the fervent anti-revisionist attitudes of the Cultural Revolution were not solely kept within the confines of China's borders. Chinese anti-revisionism also affected the ways in which PRC officials interacted with their North Vietnamese counterparts. To the point of obsession, Zhou Enlai continued to berate North Vietnamese officials about the presence of Soviet revisionists in their country. In one such conversation with Le Duan, Zhou exclaimed "the Soviets used their support to Vietnam to win your trust in a deceitful way. Their purpose is to cast a shadow over the relationship between Vietnam and China, to split Vietnam and China, with a view to further controlling Vietnam to improve [their] relations with the U.S. and obstructing the struggle and revolution of the Vietnamese people." Zhou continued and said that no Soviet volunteers or advisors should be allowed to enter Vietnam because they "may disclose secrets to the enemy."[58]

Despite this, Le Duan attended the CPSU party congress in Moscow on April 11, 1966. During the meeting, Brezhnev pledged to increase military aid to Hanoi. Two days later, in a meeting with PRC officials, Le Duan exclaimed that "you are saying that the Soviets are selling out the Vietnamese, but we don't say so." An angry PRC official named Deng Xiaoping (who as we will see had an enormous effect on postwar Sino–Vietnamese relations) retorted that Le Duan and Vietnamese leadership was "afraid of displeasing the Soviets."[59] North Vietnamese officials also began to resent the ways PRC officials would harangue them and stated that Hanoi should avoid "insulting" the PRC by publicly recognizing both Chinese and Soviet aid. Furthermore, Mao continued to pontificate from his perch in Beijing on how the North Vietnamese should conduct their war against the Americans.

After one contentious meeting between Mao, Pham Van Dong, and Vo Nguyen Giap in 1967, Hanoi began to believe that "China was willing to fight the war to the last Vietnamese."[60] The continued paranoia and chauvinism of the PRC did little to assuage relations between Beijing and Hanoi. In fact, the constant badgering emanating from PRC representatives led to Hanoi viewing Chinese involvement in Vietnam with greater skepticism. DRV officials became increasingly frustrated with what they saw as Chinese efforts to spoil any cooperation between Hanoi, Beijing, and Moscow. In essence, according to historian Nicholas Khoo, "The basic problem for the Chinese was that the Vietnamese did not view the Soviets in the same way the Chinese did."[61]

The Cultural Revolution, as stated above, also led to a severe breakdown in the PRC government's control of its own populace. Nowhere was this more evident than in some of China's border provinces with Vietnam. Guangxi province, for example, was a vital border province where trains traveling from the Soviet Union to North Vietnam had to traverse. At the height of the Cultural Revolution, Guangxi was gripped by brutal violence between competing revolutionary factions. Despite pleas from

CCP leaders such as Zhou Enlai, the violence continued well into 1968, with revolutionaries even seizing weapons from Soviet trains bound for Vietnam.[62]

One such example occurred in 1966, when a Soviet train bound for Hanoi was stopped by Chinese troops in Guangxi and crates of newly minted automatic rifles were replaced by older, worn-out Chinese rifles. In a similar incident, a train from the Soviet Union bound for North Vietnam containing the latest surface-to-air missile system was stopped, the missiles were removed and hastily dissected by Chinese technicians, and then they were hastily put back together. Their incorrect reassembly immediately gave away Chinese attempts to hide what had happened. When the issue was raised by Hanoi, PRC officials scoffed and denied the allegations.[63]

On August 22, 1967, Red Guards stopped a train at the Sino-Vietnamese border and looted thousands of Soviet-made antiaircraft rounds.[64] Additionally, Red Guards from Guangxi province began to habitually cross the border into Vietnam in search of "American imperialists" to fight. In October of 1966, high school students from Beijing and Shanghai began to cross the border and join Chinese advisors already in country. Embarrassed by mobs of children illegally crossing the sovereign border of an (albeit now-estranged) ally, Zhou Enlai declared in 1967 that all Red Guards present in Vietnam had to return to the PRC under penalty of arrest.[65] However, the damage had been done. Hanoi had grown sick of the paranoid and chaotic nature of the Cultural Revolution. With further escalation of the war in Vietnam occurring and calls for larger-scale engagements with American forces growing, the DRV's reliance on the Soviet Union for arms and support grew stronger. The biggest departure from Chinese strategy to date came in January 1968, during the Vietnamese Lunar New Year celebrations known as Tet.

The Tet Offensive of 1968 and the Tank Attack at Lang Vei

By 1968, the war in Vietnam had reached a fever pitch. Since the introduction of U.S. combat forces in March of 1965, 20,000 U.S. service members had been killed in Vietnam. ARVN losses were close to 40,000, whereas PAVN and Viet Cong had lost an estimated 230,000 troops. Political leaders in Hanoi sought to break what was rapidly becoming a stalemate. In the summer of 1967, Le Duan called together PAVN General Staff and ordered them to devise a plan for a "general offensive" and "general uprising" in the South. The plan called for PAVN and Viet Cong troops to assault the enemy's "nerve center" in South Vietnam's cities and towns. Simultaneously, PAVN planned to keep American forces isolated in parts of the South Vietnamese countryside. If this was successfully achieved, PAVN planners believed that they could easily deal with weaker ARVN forces in the cities. The American firebase at Khe Sanh was selected as a primary diversionary target aimed at drawing U.S. forces out of the cities prior to the offensive.

In October 1967, the North Vietnamese Politburo met to finalize the plans for the upcoming offensive. It was decided that the offensive would be launched on January 30, 1968, on the Tet holiday.[66] The Tet Offensive of 1968 was a major departure from PAVN tactics from years prior. While PAVN had followed a hybrid Vietnamized version of Mao's people's war strategy up until 1968, Tet was the exact inverse of Maoist strategic doctrine in two major ways. First, the emphasis on conducting a large scale, urban uprising was side-stepping the incremental approaches of a people's war strategy. To the proponents of the people's war strategy, only once the rural peasantry had been successfully mobilized and armed in force could revolutionary forces begin to launch attacks on major urban centers. Secondly, the Tet Offensive flew in the face of the Maoist approach to "protracted war." For Mao and his compatriots, a revolutionary army could not launch the "mobile war" phase of fighting unless revolutionary forces had reached an equilibrium with their enemies.

To some PRC observers, the North Vietnamese were moving too fast and had not yet achieved parity with the United States and South Vietnam.[67] However, North Vietnam did not favor the Chinese approach for several reasons, the foremost being that Hanoi in 1968 began to view continued protracted war with an emphasis on attrition against U.S. forces with greater skepticism. As mentioned previously, the 1965–67 casualty figures for the North Vietnamese had been astounding. Hanoi began to believe that the current rate of attrition was unsustainable, and that only much larger offensives aimed at inflicting much heavier casualties on U.S. forces could truly win the war. In emphasizing larger offensive actions aimed at destroying large numbers of American forces, Hanoi was inevitably leaning harder on the Soviet model of mechanized, technology-focused warfare.

From the Chinese perspective, Hanoi had committed two grievous errors in its planning for the Tet offensive. Not only had the North Vietnamese embraced a rushed and flawed strategy, but they were relying heavily on Moscow's weapons and support to do so.[68] One such weapon that made its debut on the North Vietnamese side during the Tet Offensive was the Soviet PT-76 tank. At an isolated U.S. Special Forces camp near the Marine Combat Base at Khe Sanh, PT-76 tanks caused havoc and inflicted upon the Americans and their South Vietnamese allies one of the few unequivocal victories of the Tet Offensive.

Nine days before the start of the Tet Offensive, PAVN launched a full-scale assault against the Marine Combat Base at Khe Sanh. The siege of Khe Sanh was meant to distract American forces and draw them into the South Vietnamese countryside.[69] Eight kilometers southeast of Khe Sanh was the U.S. Army Special Forces (more commonly referred to as Green Berets) camp at Lang Vei. Lying just 1.5 kilometers from the Laotian border, Lang Vei was under the control of the U.S. 5th Special Forces group. The camp was destroyed in May 1967 during a PAVN probing attack, and then subsequently rebuilt that September at a new location on Highway 9.[70] Highway 9 led directly from the Laotian border through Lang Vei, eventually reaching the Marine Combat Base at Khe Sanh. Strategically speaking, any attack on Khe Sanh had to deal with the 300 Civilian Irregular Defense Group (CIDG) personnel, 200 Montagnard tribesmen, 13 ARVN Special Forces, and 24 Green Berets stationed at Lang Vei.[71] Additionally, Lang Vei was utilized for intelligence collection, pacification, and interdiction missions throughout the immediate area. It was for these reasons that PAVN sought to seize Lang Vei.[72]

At 0530 hours on January 21, 1968, the Marine Combat Base at Khe Sanh came under rocket attack from PAVN artillery units. During the opening barrage, a rocket struck a Marine ammunition dump, severely depleting the defenders' overall ammunition count. Later that day, the nearby village of Khe Sanh (several miles from the base itself) was overrun by PAVN forces. The attack against Khe Sanh, which would last for 77 days, had begun.[73]

The Green Berets and their allies at Lang Vei knew that the actions of January 21 had put them in a precarious situation. With the capture of Khe Sanh village, PAVN had effectively cut the road between Lang Vei and the Marine Combat base. Any relief or reinforcements deployed to Lang Vei would therefore have to travel via helicopter insertion. To make matters worse, during a January reconnaissance mission along the Laotian border, Lang Vei Green Berets, alongside their Montagnard troops, discovered the unmistakable presence of tank tracks. The presence of tanks was confirmed several days later when on January 24, fleeing Laotian troops and civilians traveling down Route 9 told the Green Berets that they had come under attack by regular PAVN forces, as well as several tanks. Green Beret commanders at Lang Vei were shocked by this news.

Lang Vei only possessed two antitank rifles, though neither of them was equipped with High Explosive Anti-Tank (HEAT) rounds. Further, the presence of civilians in and around the Lang Vei camp, as well as the fact that PAVN had never used tanks in battle, prevented the deployment of antitank mines. Lastly, while Lang Vei had received a shipment of M72 LAW antitank rockets, few of the troops within the compound (outside of the 24 Green Berets) had any experience using them.

As the Marines at Khe Sanh still dodged PAVN artillery, the Special Forces soldiers at Lang Vei continued to discover signs of an imminent attack. On January 30, Green Berets patrolling along a nearby river discovered an underwater road that was invisible to aircraft and could support the weight of heavy machinery. The next day, a Montagnard patrol traversing just outside Lang Vei's wire ambushed and killed over 50 PAVN soldiers.[74] The same day, news of the Tet Offensive erupting across the cities and towns of South Vietnam reached the commanders at Lang Vei. Trouble was coming. The only question was, when?[75]

Late in the evening of February 6, 1968, the commander of Lang Vei, Captain Frank Willoughby, got word from two of his troops' defensive positions that they'd heard noises which sounded like mechanical engines revving up. Earlier that evening, fire from PAVN 152 mm artillery pieces had peppered the camp, wounding two soldiers. For the men at Lang

Vei, artillery fire was something they were used to. What came next was a horrifying confirmation of what intelligence and reconnaissance had suggested for weeks. Just after midnight on February 7, five Soviet-built PT-76 tanks followed by two platoons of PAVN infantry made their way up the road to Lang Vei. As the tanks approached, one of them detonated a trip flare which lit up the tanks for all to see.[76]

The PT-76 is a Soviet light amphibious tank that weighs 14 tons and is armed with a 76 mm main gun, as well as one 12.7 mm machine gun for antiaircraft defense and a coaxial 7.62 mm machine gun for use against enemy troops. What the PT-76 lacks in its armor (which is only 0.5 inches thick), it makes up for in speed and maneuverability (30 mph max speed).[77] While designed more for reconnaissance than heavy combat, the appearances of PT-76s at Lang Vei on the night of February 7 sealed the fate of the Special Forces camp. While factory versions of the PT-76 were lightly armored, PAVN had welded and strapped makeshift armor to

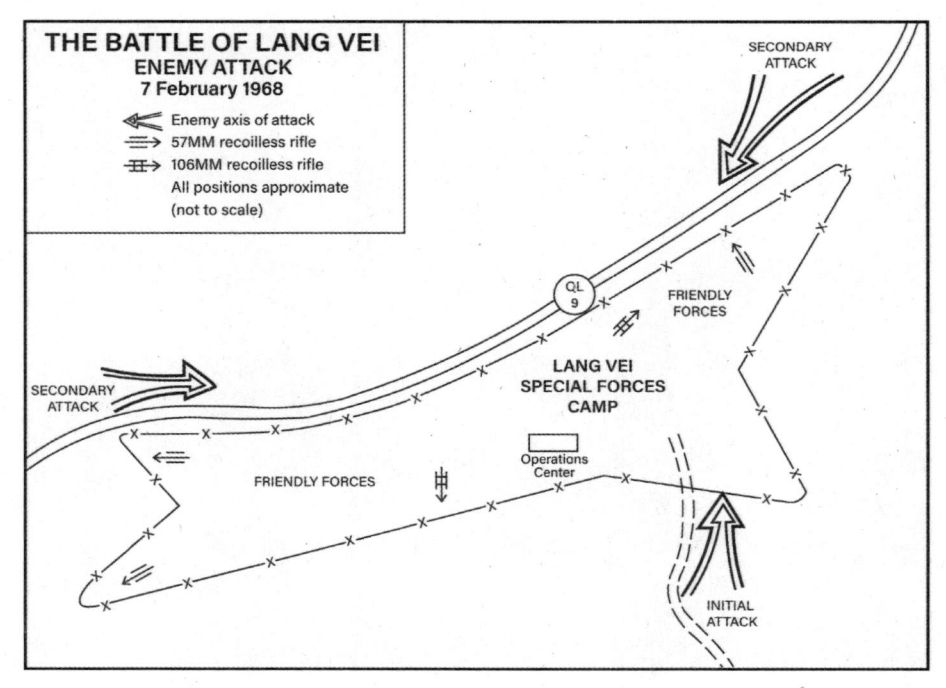

An American map highlighting PAVN routes of attack during the battle for the Lang Vei Special Forces Camp. (Wikimedia Commons/U.S. Army Center of Military History)

their tanks, making it harder for the Green Berets to successfully knock out the tanks with the weapons they had on hand.[78]

One hour into the attack at Lang Vei, the PT-76s had successfully breached the outer perimeter and were heading to the Tactical Operations Center (TOC) bunker, which was the last point of defense for the camp. Several Green Berets attempted to knock out some of the PT-76s with the M72 LAWs. To their dismay, several of the LAWs misfired. One of the LAWs was finally able to launch, but the rocket simply glanced off PAVN-improved armor of the PT-76. As Lang Vei Veteran Sergeant Major Dennis Thompson explained, "We had some 57 millimeter recoilless rifles that would have eaten those tanks up. But the team sergeant gave them to the Laotians over at the other camp. So we were dead. The LAW rockets that we had wouldn't even fire—half of them wouldn't go off. The ones that did were all over the place."[79]

While several tanks were eventually knocked out, there were still approximately nine tanks assaulting the position.[80] Despite heroic efforts

Aerial reconnaissance of the Lang Vei camp after the battle. A destroyed PAVN tank can be seen in the upper right-hand corner. (Wikimedia Commons/Colonel Thomas Pike)

by the Green Berets and those CIDG troops who had not fled at the sight of oncoming enemy armor, the PT-76s had breached the camp's inner perimeter by 0245 hours. Most of the Green Berets who were still alive at this point were cornered inside of the TOC bunker, exchanging small arms fire and grenades with PAVN and PT-76s which were now all over Lang Vei.[81] Despite repeated attempts by rescue forces to reach those trapped in the bunker, by 1110 hours it became clear to Captain Willoughby and his remaining troops that help was not coming. With the help of continued U.S. air and artillery strikes, Willoughby and two of his soldiers were able to escape the compound and link up with search-and-rescue choppers several miles away. The fight for Lang Vei was over. Out of the 24 Green Berets stationed at Lang Vei, only 3 escaped unscathed. Over 200 CIDG troops were killed during the battle. While the fall of Lang Vei did not lead to Khe Sanh Combat Base being overrun, it did mark not only the first use of enemy armor in an attack capacity, but the first successful one at that.[82]

For the most part, the Tet Offensive was a military failure for the North Vietnamese. Most of their initial seizures of key urban objectives were quickly rolled back by counterattacking U.S. and ARVN forces.[83] However, Lang Vei was a clear victory for PAVN. A U.S. Special Forces camp in a key part of South Vietnam was decisively overrun. After-action reports of the battle of Lang Vei noted a severe lack of not only antitank training, but of "psychological conditioning" when it came to facing down enemy armor. One report went on to say that "more emphasis" should be placed on antitank training for U.S., CIDG, and ARVN personnel going forward.[84]

However, during its attack on Lang Vei PAVN did commit several strategic mistakes. For example, the first two tanks to approach the compound on the night of February 7 not only turned on their headlights several times, but their commanders were sitting exposed with their hatches open. By exposing both their crews as well as themselves to enemy fire, these tank commanders could have jeopardized the entire first phase of the attack. However, since the Green Berets were not prepared for such an attack, these cardinal sins of tank tactics were not immediately punished.

While PAVN clearly picked an easy target by choosing Lang Vei, their insistence of sending in the PT-76s in scattered formations likely prolonged the battle unnecessarily.[85] Some of these problems were exposed a year later in March of 1969 at the Special Forces Camp at Ben Het. Here, several PT-76s tried to overrun a reinforced and well-armed Special Forces camp complete with American tanks. Despite a brief firefight, two PT-76s were knocked out at the cost of zero American tanks.[86] Despite this, PAVN would continue to enlarge its armored force in the years to come. This became apparent when a new American president and a new American strategy to reverse the stalemate of Vietnam called for an invasion of neighboring Laos.

Vietnamization and the Tank Battles of Operation *Lam Son 719*

While Tet was a military failure for Hanoi, it did shift the political initiative decisively in the favor of the North Vietnamese. Tet exposed to the American public that PAVN and Viet Cong were more organized and capable than military and political leaders in Washington would have

A PT-76 tank on display at the Army Museum in Hanoi. (Wikimedia Commons/Gary Todd)

them believe. Tet galvanized American public opinion regarding the Vietnam War, and public support for pursuing the war in Vietnam never recovered.[87] President Johnson, who had escalated the war in Vietnam and ordered the deployment of American combat troops, also never recovered from the shock of Tet. In March of 1968, he announced that he would not be seeking reelection in the fall. Three months later, in June, General Creighton Abrams took over command of MACV from General William Westmoreland. In November, a flailing Democratic Party lost a narrow election to Republican Richard Nixon.[88] The stage was now set for a new strategy in Vietnam that sought to extricate American forces while building up South Vietnam's armed forces.

On March 5, 1969, Secretary of Defense Melvin Laird and Chairman of the Joint Chiefs of Staff General Earl Wheeler made a trip to South Vietnam to determine the ability of the RVNAF to take over greater responsibility of fighting PAVN and Viet Cong while American forces began to withdraw. Despite protestations from General Abrams, Laird instructed Abrams to increase the training and capabilities of the RVNAF. Laird returned to the White House several days later convinced that the South Vietnamese would soon be able to take over a larger role in the war, thus giving the United States an opportunity to extricate its forces from Vietnam. On March 28, President Nixon and his chief advisors met to discuss Laird's findings and recommendations. When General Andrew Goodpaster suggested calling this new process "de-Americanizing" the war, Laird disagreed. The more appropriate term for this new strategy, he argued, was "Vietnamizing." The term "Vietnamization" was born.[89]

The Vietnamization strategy was unveiled to the American public on June 8, 1969, after a meeting between President Nixon and South Vietnamese President Nguyen Van Thieu on Midway Island in the Pacific Ocean. Privately, President Van Thieu was not pleased with the announcement for two reasons. One, it implied that prior to the announcement of this strategy, the South Vietnamese had been standing idly by while their American counterparts were taking the fight to the enemy. Second, the calls for rapid American withdrawals worried Van Thieu because it meant that one day soon, him and his countrymen would have to go it alone against PAVN and Viet Cong. Despite this, Vietnamization would go forward in three phases.

The first phase called for the bulk of the ground combat against the VC and PAVN to be conducted by the RVNAF with considerable air, naval, and logistical support provided by the United States. The second phase called for a buildup of RVNAF air, naval, and artillery capabilities so that one day they could utilize effective firepower against PAVN and VC without any American presence. The third phase involved the continued withdrawal of combat American forces, with a small number of advisors remaining behind to assist with phases one and two.[90]

The initial test of Vietnamization occurred in the spring of 1970 when U.S. and ARVN forces invaded Cambodia as a means of discovering and destroying PAVN's supplies and command location. From April to June 1970, U.S. and ARVN forces invaded and occupied the eastern border regions of Cambodia. In the process, many PAVN supplies were located and destroyed. On May 31, 1970, President Nixon called the ARVN and U.S. performance in Cambodia "visible proof of the success of Vietnamization."[91] However, the truth behind the ARVN's performance in Cambodia was more complicated. Despite some initial contact with PAVN forces, ARVN forces in Cambodia did not see prolonged, intense fighting. Also, ARVN forces showed a lack of the combined arms tactics needed to coordinate with armor, air, and infantry.[92] However, this sense of progress led to a desire amongst U.S. political and military leaders to further test Vietnamization. This time, the Ho Chi Minh Trail in Laos would be the litmus test.

The idea for a South Vietnamese-led invasion of Laos gained traction six months after the conclusion of the Cambodian incursion. In December 1970, General Abrams' plan for an ARVN attack into Laos, codenamed Operation *Lam Son 719*, was presented to and approved by the White House. The incursion would occur in four phases.

Phase one called for a U.S. mechanized brigade to re-open Route 9 into Laos (the same Route 9 that led to the now-defunct Lang Vei Camp). In phase two, ARVN armored forces, supported by heliborne infantry covering their flanks, would advance towards the Laotian village of Tchepone on Route 9, which was believed to be the logistical hub for the Laotian portion of the Ho Chi Minh Trail. Phase three involved a plan to build up the airfield at Tchepone as a means of flying in supplies to enable ARVN forces to carry out follow on attacks against PAVN.

In phase four, ARVN forces would withdraw back to South Vietnam, leaving "stay-behind" guerillas. Because of recent American legislation known as the Cooper-Church Amendment, no American ground forces were permitted to cross over the Laotian border. However, American planners were optimistic that with the presence of U.S. airpower, the ARVN would be successful.[93]

PAVN, having been set back by the Cambodian Incursion of 1970, began to bolster its forces in Laos. The 304th Division, the 308th Division, two battalions from the 202nd Tank Regiment, and one battalion from the 203rd Tank were moved into a strategic reserve position in Laos in December 1970.[94] The biggest advantage that these units had was that they were going to be fighting in areas with sound logistics and where supplies were close at hand. As PAVN official history states, there was a massive buildup of fuel and ammunition just north of Route 9 prior to the battle that was meant to serve these tank units. Continuing, the official history emphatically proclaims, "With a clear understanding of the importance of this campaign, our armored cadres and enlisted men

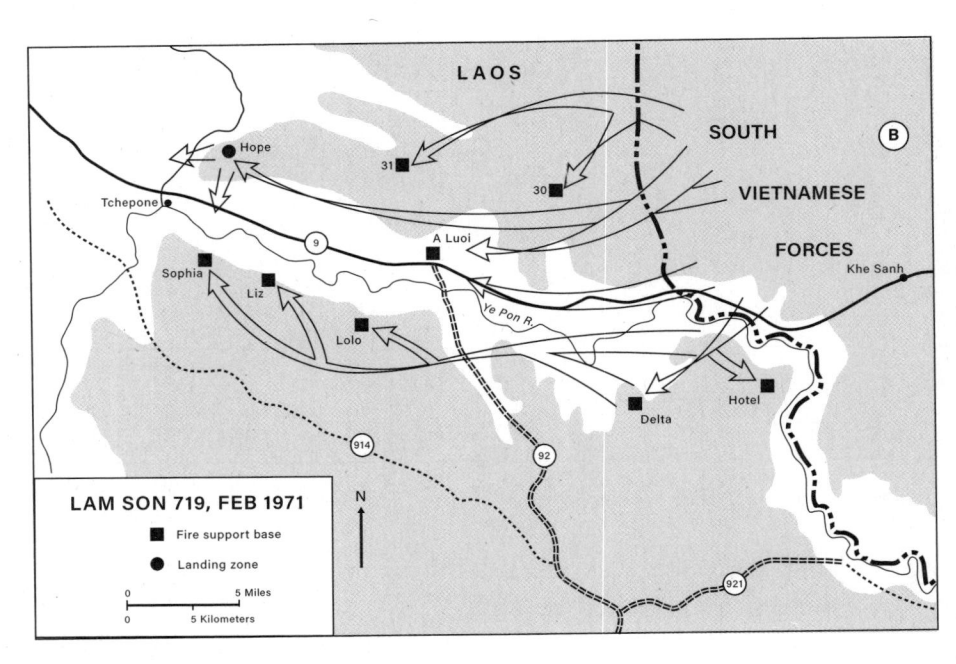

Operation *Lam Son 719* invasion routes. (Wikimedia Commons/U.S. Army)

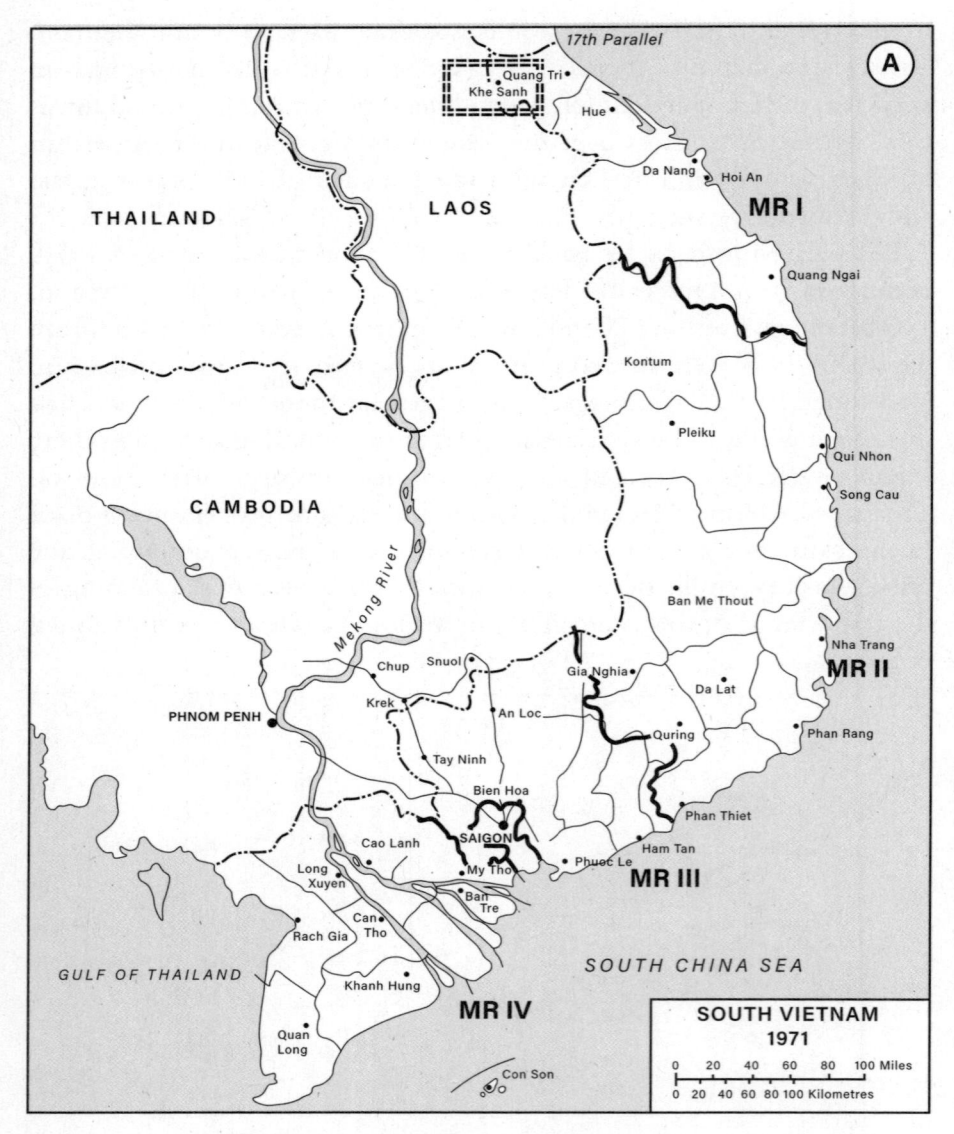

56 • ALLIANCES & ARMOR

Military Regions (MRs) within South Vietnam. (Wikimedia Commons/U.S. Army)

actively and aggressively completed the final tasks of the preparatory phase and prepared to enter the fight."[95]

The fight began on February 8 when ARVN tanks began to roll over the border into Laos. Despite intelligence suggesting that the Laotian stretch of Route 9 was adequate for armored vehicles, ARVN armored units discovered that it was "a neglected forty-year-old, single-lane road, with high shoulders on both sides and no maneuver room."[96] PAVN's response to the incursion was swift and brutal. By February 20, heliborne Landing Zone 31 had been attacked by PAVN infantry and armor. Despite fierce and temporarily successful counterattacks by ARVN armor, Landing Zone 31 was eventually lost and PAVN tanks continued to pour into the battle.[97]

It soon became clear to both the Americans and South Vietnamese that they had stepped on a hornet's nest of unforeseen magnitude. A U.S. after-action report of the Laos operation expresses near disbelief at the amount of armor, antiaircraft artillery, and large-caliber ground artillery PAVN deployed into Laos as a means of protecting its supply base. Of particular interest is a quote from the report detailing PAVN's newfound use for armor: "Heavy reliance on armor was the most striking departure from past PAVN behavior patterns. Tanks were continuously in evidence once the campaign got started and served numerous functions over the entire battle zone."[98]

Despite heavy fighting, ARVN units reached Tchepone in early March. However, PAVN had moved most of its supplies and was still continuously attacking ARVN forces all along Route 9. Despite pleas from U.S. commanders that ARVN forces should continue their search for supplies, South Vietnamese President Van Thieu ordered a withdrawal of ARVN forces from Laos.[99] What amounted to five PAVN divisions present in Laos now saw fit to chase ARVN down Route 9. One ARVN unit, the 11th Armored Cavalry, was relentlessly pursued by PAVN tank units. By the time it had reached the South Vietnamese border, the unit had lost 60 percent of its armored vehicles.[100]

Despite hopes of U.S. air support saving the day, two problems occurred. First, U.S. helicopter gunships deployed to the area could not knock out the heavily armored (especially when compared to the flimsy PT-76) Soviet T-54/55 tanks due to a lack of armor-piercing rockets.[101] Second, while fixed-wing aircraft proved to be more adept at knocking out PAVN armor, the weather in central Laos during February–March refused to cooperate. During the vicious fights for the landing zones in late February, for example, severe thunderstorms prevented the deployment of tactical air support, leaving PAVN T-54/55s advancing on ARVN landing zones virtually unmolested.[102]

The withdrawal from Laos, as well as the operation as a whole, showed that ARVN had two major shortcomings. First, it lacked a sincere sense of combined arms tactics, especially when dealing with infantry and armor. Second, ARVN still deeply relied on U.S. firepower to have a fighting chance. In short, *Lam Son 719* was a failure. It not only permanently soured President Nixon's relationship with General Creighton Abrams, but further distanced President Van Thieu from his nominal allies in Washington.[103] However, Hanoi was elated. Following *Lam Son 719*, a North Vietnamese newspaper called the disastrous withdrawal of ARVN forces proof that the "puppet soldiers" of South Vietnam were inherently weak. Furthermore, the article goes on to say that U.S. firepower was now "a prop that could no longer be relied on."[104] The confidence that Hanoi gained following *Lam Son 719* led to major events in 1972 that, in most estimations, did not go according to plan.

As the war in Vietnam escalated with the introduction of American airpower and later American ground troops, the dynamics of Hanoi's dual strategies for military conflict as well as international relations shifted. For the Soviet Union, the escalation of America's war in Vietnam happened occurred as the former was experiencing a shakeup in its country's leadership. The ascension of Leonid Brezhnev to the USSR's highest office led to a massive shift in his country's policy towards Vietnam. No longer would the Soviet Union sit idly by as Vietnam suffered under the weight of American aggression. Simultaneously, Soviet attempts at rekindling cordial relations with the PRC faltered dramatically, thus giving further incentive for Brezhnev to cozy up to Hanoi in a bid to win the allegiance of the North Vietnamese Politburo.

For the PRC, Mao's continued attempts to make his nation the shining path of proletarian revolution faltered, ruining his nation's standing both domestically and internationally. The excesses of the Cultural Revolution not only destabilized the PRC itself, but it also destabilized the country's relations with North Vietnam. The hijacking of Soviet arms shipments, as well as the blatant disregard for Vietnamese sovereignty when Chinese schoolchildren marched to Hanoi, had a drastically negative effect on Sino-Vietnamese relations. Furthermore, the PRC's anger over the fact that the North Vietnamese would not adopt a strict, by-the-book Maoist war strategy after 1964 widened the gap between Hanoi and Beijing.

For Hanoi, a combination of the shift in Soviet and Chinese attitudes towards North Vietnam from 1964–71 and American escalation led to drastic shifts in the Politburo's approaches to war strategy. While Resolution 9 had laid the groundwork in 1963, the conclusion of the Politburo's meeting of October 1967 marked a drastic shift in Hanoi's war strategy. Gone were the days of lightly armed yet highly capable mobile infantry units operating solely in rural areas. Instead, increasingly mechanized and heavily armed PAVN units assaulted urban areas during Tet. The increased reliance on Soviet technologies such as the PT-76 tank, T-54/55 tank, and modern heavy artillery led to bigger battles and bigger gambles.

While Tet was a military loss, it became a political game changer. The success of PAVN armor at Lang Vei in 1968 was a precursor to an even more mechanized version of Hanoi's army. By 1971, the mechanization and modernization within PAVN shocked even American intelligence officials. The Laotian Incursion, the purest test of Vietnamization to date, floundered as ARVN troops were routed from Tchepone all the way to the South Vietnamese border. PAVN T-54/55 tanks, a heavier, more capable model of Soviet tank, proved to be more than a match for ARVN armored forces who still heavily relied on American airpower. The stage was set for a conflagration in 1972 that, like Tet, would alter the course of the Vietnam War.

CHAPTER 3

The Easter Offensive (1972)

Détente and the Preparations for the Easter Offensive

The beginnings of what became known as the Easter Offensive started in 1971. In the North Vietnamese Politburo, there was persistent debate about what a strategy for final victory should look like. General Secretary of the Communist Party Le Duan and General Vo Nguyen Giap favored a "regular force" strategy with conventional forces. This ran counter to the "political struggle" approach of North Vietnamese officials such a Le Duc Tho, Truong Chinh, and Pham Hung. This latter group of individuals favored more negotiations and diplomacy rather than large-scale offensive military action. The previous three years of "regular force strategy" had inflicted over 600,000 casualties on the North Vietnamese. However, Le Duan's embrace of regular force strategy tipped the scales in favor of a more aggressive push for victory.[1]

On the world stage, President Richard Nixon's announcement of a trip to China, as well as China's simultaneous desire to "enhance its image within the international community," worried North Vietnamese officials and military commanders. If the United States could reach agreements with Beijing and Moscow (North Vietnam's two biggest sponsors), then the North Vietnamese struggle for unification might be swept aside.[2] As previously discussed, the PRC began to view Soviet Imperialism, following the invasion of Czechoslovakia, as the chief threat to Chinese sovereignty. In many respects, the Chinese Cultural Revolution was launched as a means of protecting China from what Mao saw as Soviet "revisionist" attitudes.[3]

By 1969, the fervor between the two nations had reached such an intensity that Mao Zedong openly warned the citizens of the PRC that a Soviet invasion of China was not only possible, but that those citizens residing in the Sino-Soviet border regions should prepare for war.[4] Seeing an opportunity to take advantage of the now-fractured relationship between Moscow and Beijing, the Nixon administration sought to establish overtures with both communist nations in the hopes that a reproachment with Mao Zedong and Leonid Brezhnev could help the Unites States extricate its forces from Vietnam. Starting in 1969, the Nixon administration expressed this desire through interlocutors such as Nicolae Ceaușescu's Romania. In a meeting with Zhou Enlai on September 7, 1969, Romanian diplomats expressed President Nixon's personal desire to see Sino-American relations improve, despite previous Cold War concerns.[5]

These overtures from Nixon were well-received by Mao for several reasons. Historian Chen Jian explains that by 1969, the Cultural Revolution in the PRC had run its course. The anti-American sentiments present within the revolution's slogans and cadres emerged at a time when Mao sought to curb the excesses of the Cultural Revolution and consolidate the gains made. Additionally, open exchanges of hostile fire along the Sino-Soviet border at Zhenbao Island in March of 1969 solidified Chinese accusations that the Soviet Union had become a "social-imperialist country," and the number one threat to Chinese national security.[6]

In September 1969, four Chinese marshals issued a report to the CCP central committee entitled "Our Views of the Current Situation." In the report, the authors concluded that the "U.S. imperialists," despite their actions in Vietnam, did not desire to see a full-blown conflict between the Soviet Union and the PRC. Especially if that conflict led to a Soviet victory. The report went on to say that the Soviet Union was the clear and immediate threat to the PRC: "A group of adventurers in the Soviet revisionist leadership want to seize this opportunity to use missiles and tanks to launch a quick war against China and thoroughly destroy China, so that a 'mortal danger' for them will be removed." The report concluded that a rapprochement with the United States could help prevent a conflict with the Soviet Union, while at the same time opening up new avenues of opportunity: "The U.S. imperialists have suggested resuming the Sino–American ambassadorial talks, to which we should respond positively when the timing is proper. Such tactical actions may bring about results of strategic significance."[7] This report for the Central Committee solidified the PRC's new strategy for achieving both increased national security along its northern border as well as a possible welcoming into the global community.

Despite protests and delays associated with the US incursion into Cambodia in May 1970 and the later South Vietnamese incursion into Laos in February 1971, both Washington and Beijing wished to continue to explore the possibilities associated with an overall cooling of tensions. In a National Security Council memorandum published at the height of the Laos Incursion entitled "NSSM 106," the Nixon administration outlined its short- and long-term goals in reaching a rapprochement with the PRC. Foremost among these goals was the hope that such an understanding with Beijing would further "prevent an offensive alliance between Peking [Beijing] and Moscow directed against the US or its Asian friends and allies," including South Vietnam.[8]

For China, the events in Laos and Cambodia were a setback, but they were not poison pills that aimed to torpedo increased Sino-American cooperation in Asia. As South Vietnamese forces poured into Laos, PRC Deputy Foreign Minister Chiao Kuan Hua approached Norway's ambassador in Beijing, Ole Aalgarrd. Chiao expressed disappointment at the increased military action in Indochina, largely on the grounds that it made further Sino-American discussions impossible for the time being. The PRC, Chiao explained to Aalgarrd, needed to maintain public solidarity with North Vietnam, and therefore could not be seen holding diplomatic talks with American officials while PAVN forces fought an American-backed incursion into Laos. However, Chiao explicitly stated that "the Chinese and the Americans nevertheless must sooner or later sit down and straighten out our relationships."[9]

Five months later on July 9, 1971, American and PRC officials did just that. United States National Security Advisor Henry Kissinger sat down with PRC prime minister and jack-of-all-trades, Zhou Enlai. Prior to their meeting, there was consternation amongst PRC officials as to how to simultaneously conduct prosperous Sino–American negotiations while maintaining good relations with the North Vietnamese. Officials within the CCP feared that improved relations with the Americans would undermine North Vietnamese efforts on the battlefield and at the ongoing peace negotiations in Paris.[10]

Zhou Enlai, realizing that upcoming talks with the Americans would undoubtedly unsettle the North Vietnamese, reassured Pham Van Dong and Le Duan in a meeting on March 7 that the PRC supported the North Vietnamese in their struggle against the newly christened "Nixon doctrine." Zhou went on to say that "not to support the revolution of the Vietnamese people is like betraying the revolution. At the same time, we are also prepared to render our sacrifices in case the enemy expands the war."[11] In an attempt to further assuage the fears and concerns of their Vietnamese allies, the PRC issued a "protocol on the provision of supplementary military equipment and materials" to Hanoi a mere five days before Kissinger's visit. While this protocol would greatly increase Chinese military aid to North Vietnam in the months leading up to the Easter Offensive, it did little to mend an already-fractured relationship with Hanoi.[12]

The meetings between the PRC and the United States between 1971–72 were profound in their initiative as well as their accomplishments. Starting with the initial meeting with Kissinger in July 1971, the PRC sought to continue to expand its relationship with the United States, with Zhou Enlai professing Mao's eagerness to meet with President Nixon in Beijing. Kissinger, in a rather profound reversal of U.S. strategic policy that had in part brought American troops to Vietnam several years prior, declared that "it is the conviction of President Nixon that a strong and developing People's Republic of China poses no threat to any essential U.S. interest." The July conversation between Kissinger and Zhou ended with a pledge to a future U.S. visit by President Richard Nixon.[13]

This visit eventually came in February 1972, one month prior to the beginning of the Easter Offensive. While there were minor flare-ups regarding issues such as Taiwan, the meeting was considered a success by both negotiating parties. In sum, Beijing and Washington had reached an understanding that events in Vietnam, so long as the Nixon administration continued to withdraw American forces, would not hinder increased relations between the two parties.[14] Interestingly, Henry Kissinger shared classified intelligence information with a Chinese general during the proceedings. The intelligence outlined Soviet troop movements along the Sino-Soviet border, and was apparently so classified that, according to Kissinger, many Senior U.S. intelligence officials had not seen it.[15]

At the conclusion of the momentous Sino-American summit in Beijing, the two parties issued what would become known as the "Shanghai Communique" on February 27, 1972. The communique clearly stated that neither the United States or PRC "should seek hegemony in the Asia-Pacific region and each is opposed to efforts by any other country or group of countries to establish such hegemony."[16] According to historian Qiang Zhai, this crucial clause in the communique "constituted an implicit expression of objection to Soviet (or Soviet-North Vietnamese) intentions."[17]

As Sino-American relations were being mended in the months leading up to the Easter Offensive, so too were relations between Washington and Moscow. While not nearly as drastic and geopolitically shattering as the administration's overtures to the PRC, President Nixon wished to improve Soviet-American relations as a means of cooling general Cold War tensions, and (as with China) as a means of helping end U.S. involvement in Vietnam. Early in the Nixon presidency, in February 1969, the president and his national security advisor, Henry Kissinger, conducted a lengthy conversation with Soviet Ambassador Anatoly Dobrynin about possible cooperation regarding arms limitation. During the meeting, Dobrynin himself suggested that arms-limitation talks could coincide with efforts to deescalate the war in Vietnam.[18]

Backchannel communications between Moscow and Washington following this meeting were bogged down by the Soviet Politburo's cumbersome approval procedure, as well as by Nixon and Kissinger's emphasis on Vietnam rather than arms control and West Berlin. Suspecting that these conflicting priorities would prevent fruitful outcomes, Soviet Foreign Minister Andrei Gromyko advised the rest of the Soviet Politburo to avoid rushing into negotiations with the Americans. It would take two years before the Soviets would continue their dialogue with the United States.

The border clashes of 1969, Nixon's proposed visit to China, and a personal overture to Soviet leader Leonid Brezhnev himself by the US president on August 5, 1971, forced the Soviets to reconsider their cold shouldering of Washington.[19] In the letter, Nixon assured Brezhnev that the previous overtures to the PRC contained no hidden motives, nor should they seek to alarm Moscow. Nixon goes on to address the situation in Southeast Asia: "I would hope that the Soviet Union would exercise its influence to achieve peace in that area of the world. Such an action would give a great impetus to the policies of reconciliation we intend to pursue." Nixon's letter ended by recognizing that, while the Soviet government has its own interests, those interests could be pursued jointly with those of the United States.[20]

This letter set in motion a course of events that eventually led to the formal announcement on October 12, 1971, that President Nixon would travel to Moscow to conduct a summit with Brezhnev with the stated main objective of a new arms limitation treaty. The projected date of the Moscow Summit was set for mid- to late May 1972.[21] Unbeknownst to the Nixon administration, but known to Moscow, May 1972 would land right in the middle of North Vietnam's planned Easter Offensive.

The diplomatic coups of the Nixon administration in 1971 were a complete shock to Le Duan and the North Vietnamese government. Almost immediately after seeing Henry Kissinger during their initial meeting in July 1971, Zhou Enlai flew to Hanoi to assuage the anger and confusion that news of the meeting fomented within the North Vietnamese government. While few parts of this conversation have been preserved, a statement to Zhou Enlai by North Vietnamese leader Le Duan probably best encapsulates his country's anger over the PRC's unexpected overtures with the United States: "In the war of aggression against Vietnam, the US goes from one surprise to another. Until the withdrawal of troops is completed, Nixon will be unable to expect what surprise is next. So the visit of Kissinger is designed to forestall these surprises."[22] While it is unclear what exactly these "surprises" were, it is reasonable to assume that the upcoming spring–summer" offensive of 1972 was at the forefront of Le Duan's mind.

Perhaps one of the biggest frustrations within the North Vietnamese government was the seeming hypocrisy that the PRC had engaged in on the world stage. In 1968, during the height of the Chinese Cultural Revolution, Mao Zedong, Zhou Enlai, and others within the PRC's government had criticized North Vietnamese leaders for engaging in peace talks and concessions with the United States. PRC Military Commander Chen Yi famously chastised North Vietnamese diplomat and negotiator Le Duc Tho for contradicting the prestige and principles of Ho Chi Minh by engaging with the Americans.[23] Ironically, Chen Yi was one of the signatories of the 1970 "four marshals" report, which encouraged the PRC to engage in rapprochement with the United States.

Internally, Le Duan and other North Vietnamese leaders fumed at the diplomatic maneuvers of the Nixon administration, as well as Beijing's and Moscow's willingness to accommodate the Americans. However, public criticism of either Chinese or Soviet leadership could possibly spell doom for Hanoi's war efforts. Up until this point, the North Vietnamese had deftly navigated the ever-widening split between its two communist patrons. By denouncing one—or even worse, both—of its benefactors, Hanoi stood to lose a significant amount of political, military, and economic support. Therefore, Hanoi remained quiet while planning for the upcoming offensive that would hopefully, in Le Duan's eyes, break the military and diplomatic deadlock before Moscow and Beijing became too warm with the United States.[24]

Archival documents suggest that there was a very strong sense of overconfidence in North Vietnam in the weeks leading up to the Easter Offensive. One such government document, entitled "Grasp the Strategic Opportunity," claimed that South Vietnam's economic, and military strength, had been greatly weakened by the departure of American ground troops. The "puppet regime," as this document refers to the South Vietnamese government, had been "suffering an extremely serious crisis in the economic, political, and social fields" in the urban and rural areas it claimed control over. Furthermore, the memo stated that the moment contained "all the favorable circumstances which may help us win this war have also increased at the present time."[25] This is the most revealing part of the document. It clearly states that the North Vietnamese intended for the Easter Offensive to win the war flat out by toppling the South Vietnamese government.

Preparation for the Nguyễn Huệ Offensive, as it was called in North Vietnam, began with an all-encompassing recruitment campaign. The previous three years of fighting had depleted the reserves of PAVN. This new recruitment campaign began to target those North Vietnamese who had previously been shielded from conscription: university students, sons of party members, teachers, and the siblings of those who had already been sent south. Students at Hanoi's Polytechnical College were told that "if graduation is not attained now, it will be done at a later time, while this is the only time to fight the Americans. The Fatherland is calling, the front lines are waiting."[26] As the manpower of PAVN was being replenished, its equipment was also being upgraded.

The months leading up to and following the Easter Offensive saw some of the biggest increases in military aid to North Vietnam of the war thus far. In 1971 both the Soviets and the Chinese increased their military aid to North Vietnam to levels not seen since 1967. In 1970, for example, combined Chinese and Soviet military aid to Hanoi amounted to $130 million. A year later, that number had spiked to $235 million. It is important to note, however, that three-fifths of this aid came from the Soviet Union.[27] In December 1971, Soviet President Nikolai Podgorny traveled to Hanoi and promised "additional aid without reimbursement." One facet of this aid came in the form of Soviet-built T-54 tanks. Simply designed and with questionable reliability issues, the T-54 nonetheless provided a new and potent arrow in the quiver of Giap's regular force strategy. And to compensate for a lack of familiarity with armored warfare, the Soviets provided advanced armor training to 3,000 North Vietnamese tank crews.[28]

However, this training itself was not particularly effective. Prisoner interrogations of PAVN tankers illustrate that North Vietnamese tank crewmen participating in the Easter Offensive had graduated from the Soviet Armored School in Odessa after a mere four to five months training. Prior to this training, few of these newly minted tank crews had seen any sort of combat.[29] On top of rushed training in the USSR, a concerning proportion of crews were given even less training in North Vietnam, as well as in staging areas in Laos and Cambodia. Such was the case with PAVN T-54 Tank946. From January 1968 until November

1971, tank 946 had largely sat in a depot and had only acquired nine hours of drive time. It was later destroyed while serving in the 203rd Armored Regiment at An Loc.[30] Another PAVN tank, Tank 341 which served with the 203rd Armored Regiment, sat in a hangar from January 1966–February 1970. Every month, Tank 341 was turned on for a total of 10 minutes for "anti-rust" maintenance.[31] This ran counter to stated PAVN training objectives for tank crews. In captured documents, PAVN cadres called for tank crew trainees to drive their respective tanks "500 times with tanks being run for a total of 1,141 hours."[32]

As historian Stephen Randolph points out, the training given to North Vietnamese tank crews proved to be "incredibly meager by Western standards."[33] Leading up to the offensive, the 397th had practiced driving and repairing its new T-54/55 tanks for a mere 10 days from January 31–February 9, 1972. Two days later, the 397th departed for battle.[34] As more men of the 397th arrived in their respective assembly areas, many fell ill with diseases such as malaria, making their training and preparation schedules even more difficult to follow. Additionally, those who were able to train and prepare for the upcoming offensive were shocked to see T-54s rather than previous, more familiar models of Soviet tanks:

> Upon arriving at the assembly area, all cadre and soldiers had to immediately receive tanks even though most of them were sick. As a result, they met with difficulties in driving K1 tanks. Being familiar with driving the K2 (PT76 amphibious tanks), almost all cadre and soldiers felt strange driving the K1 (T54 tank). Therefore, they had to spend a long time practicing to drive it well.

While select groups of North Vietnamese had received specialized tank training in the Soviet Union, there were many armored units would be seeing and driving their newly issued T-54/55s for the first time.[35] This, along with the fact that the already mechanically unreliable T-54/55s had barely been driven over the past three to five years, proved to be detrimental to PAVN's upcoming offensive. International political considerations and Politburo infighting took precedence over military and strategic preparedness. Raw recruits drawn from the professional classes of North Vietnam were thrust into battle without significant or adequate training.

A translated document of a PAVN report regarding the activities of the 1st Battalion, 203rd Armored Regiment also shows a lack of professionalism amongst the raw recruits who had been deployed to conduct the Easter Offensive. The document shows a general lack of enthusiasm and morale amongst these recruits, as well as some PAVN cadres. Often feigning illness or family difficulties, some soldiers refused to partake in duties assigned to them. More alarmingly, some soldiers refused to follow orders and did not prepare their units for movement. Thus, PAVN document concluded, "the coordination among tanks in combat was still poor. The internal solidarity was not strengthened."[36] This lack of training and morale proved to be a severe hindrance during the Easter Offensive.

The Easter Offensive and PAVN Armor Performance

The Easter Offensive was launched on March 30, 1972, with massive amounts of Soviet-supplied artillery and, of course, T-54/55 tanks. However, soon after the beginning of the offensive, cracks in the ability of PAVN to launch effective armored thrusts began to appear all over the battlespace. On April 9, for example, seven PAVN T-54s were engaged by ARVN M48 tanks at the crucial MR-1 city of Dong Ha. A summation of the events that followed was provided in an intelligence report to Military Assistance Command Vietnam (MACV):

> When taken under fire, the enemy exhibited confusion as three of the tanks veered off into a rice paddy where they subsequently became bogged down. All seven of the T-54's fired no more than a total of a dozen rounds during the entire action during which all were eventually destroyed by friendly tank fire.

Only one of the ARVN M48s sustained damage, and even that was minor. The panic displayed by PAVN T-54s in this engagement suggests a profound lack of training.[37] Dale Andradé's book *Trial by Fire* also points out a lack of combined arms training:

> [North Vietnamese] infantry, artillery, and armor were poorly coordinated, particularly in Kontum and An Loc. Tanks were usually sent into action without adequate infantry support, bogging down in the rubble-strewn streets where they were vulnerable to anti-tank weapons.[38]

PAVN would lose 23 T-54 tanks at An Loc alone.[39] ARVN General Tran Van Nhut echoes this assessment in his book *An Loc: The Unfinished War*. Van Nhut was the Binh Long provincial commander of South Vietnamese Regional/Popular Defense Forces (RF/PF). His account examines key factors regarding PAVN's use of armor during the Easter Offensive. Van Nhut's book, like others, describes the fact that there was little-to-no communication and coordination between PAVN infantry and PAVN armored units. Additionally, Van Nhut claims that PAVN forces were overly optimistic when planning the offensive and predicted that informants in places like An Loc would guide the way for their armored forces. This proved not to be the case, as PAVN tank crews clumsily drove into rubble-strewn streets making wrong turns and falling prey to RF/PF and ARVN antitank personnel. Van Nhut also points out significant problems in PAVN command-and-control structure.[40]

A training memorandum from the 9th VC Division echoes some of Van Nhut's assessment. Published shortly after the start of the Easter Offensive, the memorandum entitled "Determined to Completely Defeat the Enemy During the Nguyen Hue Campaign" highlights some of the successes and failures of PAVN/VC forces. In the "failures" section of the memorandum, it is noted that many PAVN/VC forces had failed to "apply proper combat tactics in attacking and encircling enemy troops." The memorandum also says that tactics involving the destruction and occupying enemy territory "were not proper." Perhaps the most telling part of this document is the admission that coordination between branches of PAVN's armed forces was significantly lacking.[41]

The story of Sergeant Luom at the Dong Ha bridge deserves to be reexamined as another example of poor PAVN armor performance. In his book *The Easter Offensive*, Gerald Turley chronicles the events that happened on Easter Sunday 1972 at Dong Ha. At this point, the North Vietnamese offensive was in its fourth day and the outlook for U.S. and ARVN forces looked exceedingly grim. ARVN forces were slow to deploy effectively into defensive positions in Dong Ha. The key road junction of Route 9 and Highway 1 lay just beyond Dong Ha's vital bridge, with only a battalion of ARVN marines standing in the way of a PAVN armored thrust. The mere rumor of tanks prior to their appearance on the Dong Ha battlefield had caused an entire ARVN regiment, the

57th, to flee in panic. However, Sgt. Luom and his marines stood fast and manned their positions at the bridge, despite inconsistent air support and weak armor support.[42]

What happened next, as covered in the introduction, is confirmed by an after-action report submitted by a U.S. Marine advisor on the ground at Dong Ha. At 1015 that morning, the first PAVN tanks appeared at the Dong Ha bridge. Three separate rocket teams engaged the first enemy tank as it began to cross the bridge. Because the tank was in partial cover, seven rockets were immediately fired. All of them missed their targets. However, an eighth rocket (presumably fired by Sgt. Luom) struck the tank, partially disabling it and forcing it back in the direction from whence it came.[43] In the words of Turley, "in performing this heroic act, he [Luom] provided critically needed time for the two U.S. advisors, who were on their way to the bridge to somehow prepare it for destruction."[44] While Sgt. Luom's actions were indeed heroic, the fact that a 95-pound ARVN marine could blunt a major armored advance along a crucial bridge during the high point of PAVN's offensive in MR-1 shows a profound lack of command and control amongst PAVN forces.

In *Abandoning Vietnam*, Jim Willbanks chronicles initial PAVN success followed by failure. Willbanks provides an account of the entire Easter Offensive ranging from the fighting in and around Quang Tri in MR-1 to ARVN's gamble to reopen highway 13 in MR-3. *Abandoning Vietnam* describes how the initial PAVN attacks into South Vietnam on March 30, 1972, were met with panic, in many instances, by ARVN soldiers. In MR-1, PAVN units seized key ARVN positions at Camp Carroll and Mai Loc. Similarly, in MR-3, PAVN units seized two ARVN firebases, as well as the border town of Loc Ninh, in the opening days of the offensive.

Despite these initial successes, as Willbanks points out, several factors hindered continued PAVN battlefield success. Willbanks does address the fact that PAVN severely lacked combined arms tactics and deployed armored forces without infantry support. This allowed ARVN units to knock out PAVN tanks with man-portable antitank weapons such as the M72, thus greatly increasing the morale of South Vietnamese troops (especially at places like An Loc). However, Willbanks makes it clear that he believes that US airpower played the most pivotal role in stopping PAVN attacks.

Interestingly, Willbanks also mentions that at places like An Loc, for example, PAVN forces were still able to push through continued U.S. airpower and nearly seize key command-and-control posts.[45] Willbanks' emphasis on airpower does not explain adequately how PAVN tanks were still able to break through ARVN lines and threaten to win the battle. In *The Battle of An Loc*, Willbanks only briefly touches on the training received by PAVN armor units. Willbanks admits that ARVN performance during the battle had been "uneven at best," poking a hole in the suggestion that ARVN resistance alone blunted the Easter Offensive. Willbanks also mentions, though only briefly, the lack of PAVN command-and-control prowess as well as combined arms training. However, he devotes the majority of one chapter, "Evaluating the Battle of An Loc," to U.S. airpower statistics.[46]

In his book *Vietnam: An Epic Tragedy*, Hastings touches on several instances where PAVN armor failed to make significant breakthroughs, he

ARVN soldiers atop a captured PAVN tank during the 1972 Easter Offensive. This photo was taken in the immediate vicinity of Dong Ha. (Wikimedia Commons/U.S. Army Center of Military History)

places significant emphasis on the events at An Loc. Echoing Willbanks' assessment, PAVN tank crews hopelessly and ineffectively moved their armored forces into An Loc. On April 13, 1972, several T-54s advanced into An Loc alone and, once again, without infantry support. One tank fell into a ditch while its companions were "destroyed piecemeal by LAW rockets and air strikes."[47] However a particular quote from U.S. advisor Captain Hal Moffett after the April 13 battle highlights an interesting analysis:

> [The communists] didn't use their tanks properly, and thank God for that. If they had used a good coordinated attack they would have rolled right on through, but they were completely disorganized and till this day I don't understand what they were trying to do with the tanks sending in four or five at a time.[48]

The interesting aspect of this quote is that a seasoned advisor acknowledged that the initial armored offensive at An Loc could have succeeded with proper tactics. Despite the presence of ARVN armed with M72 LAW as well as overwhelming U.S. air support, it was incredibly possible that PAVN could have achieved a breakthrough at An Loc during the opening weeks of the Easter Offensive.[49]

Furthering this suggestion, PAVN armor did in fact achieve major breakthroughs at the outset of the offensive. ARVN Lieutenant General Ngo Quang Truong, for example, notes several instances where PAVN tanks succeeded in breaking through ARVN defenses. On April 2, 1972, PAVN launched the second prong of its Easter Offensive into MR-3 in the Binh Long province of South Vietnam. The key ARVN fire support base of Lac Long fell within hours in the face of oncoming enemy tanks. By midday on April 2, the base was captured by PAVN.[50] It was also during this time, Truong notes, that U.S. airpower had effectively been taken out of the fight. During the opening salvos of the Easter Offensive, prolonged inclement weather prevented US and ARVN forces from effectively deploying tactical air support.[51] Because of this, key ARVN positions in MR-1 such as Camp Carroll fell quickly in the face on PAVN's onslaught.[52]

However, Truong also chronicles the very shortcomings that would eventually undo PAVN's offensive. In his conclusion, Truong notes "that all PAVN tactical commanders lacked experience in the employment of armor."[53] Truong mentions that PAVN did not adequately foresee nor prepare for the known difficulties of deploying armor in some of the more remote parts of South Vietnam. Additionally, PAVN did not utilize its armor to exploit the victories won at the outset of the offensive. Rather than push the attack and make deep thrusts into enemy territory, PAVN used their tanks hesitantly and piecemeal. Truong exclaims "Kontum and An Loc also might have been more vulnerable to the enemy if the initial momentum had been sustained."[54]

The events leading up to and including the attacks at Kontum over a month into the Easter Offensive also reflect serious shortcomings in PAVN armored tactics. On the evening (2230) of May 13, 1972, US advisors and ARVN personnel manning defensive positions in Kontum noticed headlights moving down Highway 14. What were initially thought to be the headlights of PAVN supply trucks heading straight towards ARVN positions turned out to be columns of T-54 tanks moving into attack positions. A US advisor present for this bizarre event could only speculate that, due to PAVN's inexperience in moving tanks even in the best of circumstances, local PAVN commanders had decided to turn on the tanks' headlights so as to best position their forces. All this despite the fact that such a risky maneuver invited artillery and air support to swoop in and destroy this blundering column of armor.

The PAVN attack the next morning saw PAVN infantry separate from their accompanying tanks as soon as artillery fire was called in. This enabled ARVN "tank-killer" teams to knock out these T-54s before air support was even brought to bear. The poor armored-warfare tactics of PAVN once again prevented significant gains on a vital sector of battlefront.[55] At one point during the battle for Kontum, so many destroyed enemy tanks littered the battlefield that local U.S. advisors lost count of how many had actually been destroyed on a day-by-day basis.[56]

PAVN's inability to utilize their armor effectively was not noticed solely by ARVN and US forces. North Vietnamese Deputy Chief of the General Staff Lieutenant General Tran Van Quang, for example, acknowledged "a lack of high-quality tactical training and combat experience." Going further, Quang expressed disappointment that PAVN tank crews "did not correctly apply the principle of conducting massed armored attacks against the primary targets in key battles."[57] In the same speech given to members of the Soviet Politburo, Van Quang expresses disappointment in PAVN command staff and its poor execution of directives and orders issued by the Supreme High Command in Hanoi. Contrary to North Vietnamese propaganda disseminated to the public, Van Quang admitted to his Soviet counterparts that PAVN had suffered over 140,000 casualties, including the loss of 264 tanks across the battlefront. When explaining the significant loss of armored forces, Van Quang said that it was not solely due to American airpower: "In addition, as experience shows, we still have not sufficiently established a clear system of command and control of our forces."[58]

This sentiment is also expressed in *Victory in Vietnam: The Official History of the People's Army of Vietnam, 1954–1975*. This book, written by the Military History Institute of Vietnam, sheds light on some of the thinking and PAVN tactics that shaped the Easter Offensive. While the book is heavily biased, there are a few key admissions that shed light on some of the persistent failures associated with PAVN's conduction of the Easter Offensive. One such glaring admission has to do with North Vietnamese command and control. "Because of deficiencies in our command organization," *Victory in Vietnam* argues, "we [PAVN] usually missed our opportunities [to pursue withdrawing ARVN forces]." Revealing its bias, however, the book goes on to describe PAVN's hastily put together combined arms offensive as the "correctly selected offensive methods."[59]

Directly contradicting the direct emphasis on U.S. airpower is a PAVN memorandum issued in May of 1972. This memorandum explains and analyzes PAVN's failure to capture the vital city of An Loc, referred to as the "primary mission" of communist forces in the surrounding area. In the memorandum, there is little-to-no mention of U.S. airpower and its effect on advancing PAVN forces. Rather, this memo is clear as to why attempts to seize An Loc had failed:

> Consequently, we have not yet satisfied the expectations of all cadre and soldiers on the Route 13 front and other battlefields, as well as those in the rear and on the front lines.... The reasons for our failure to overrun the HQ [An Loc] are due to our deficiencies in leadership, command, organization, combat actions, and coordination among armed services.[60]

Of particular interest in this quote is the inclusion of "combat actions" and "coordination among armed services." A deficiency in "combat actions" reveals that PAVN forces were unable to capitalize on battlefield opportunities. It also suggests a lack of effective combat training that later manifested itself on a critical front of the Easter Offensive.

A report from MACV dated November 1972 also highlights the lack of training of PAVN tank crews. The report chronicles the history of PAVN's armor command. Starting in 1959, PAVN's armor command largely trained crews on captured French colonial tanks such as the M-24 Chaffee. It took until 1967 for PAVN to acquire a fleet of modern Soviet tanks. Furthermore, these new tanks were used strictly in a defensive posture for the first four years of their deployment. In 1971, PAVN tanks were finally used (though only short-term) in significant numbers outside of North Vietnam. During 1971's ARVN incursion into Laos, PAVN tanks were used to counterattack and throw back invading ARVN forces.

The report goes on to describe the training PAVN armored forces received prior to the Easter Offensive. Very little of what was taught at PAVN armor schools was practiced or rehearsed prior to deployment. In a shocking revelation, the report states "school trained tank crews often fire their first rounds in battle." The report goes on to emphasize that while trained in Soviet combined arms tactics, PAVN's failure to rehearse these tactics meant that they would not be employed during combat.[61] This report shows that the rush to field a conventional force in support of the Easter Offensive led to the deployment of an ill-trained armored fighting force who had not even fired tank cannons on a training range. The "baptism of fire" these trainees faced on the battlefields of the Easter Offensive were harsh and jarring.

A study of the Easter Offensive published by the Intelligence Directorate of MACV in January 1973 highlighted that not only did PAVN tank crews receive poor training, but their command-and-control structure also hindered their chances at success. According to the report, "armored units were generally attached to infantry units and therefore were controlled by infantry division, regimental and battalion commanders."[62] The report went on to say that these infantry officers did not receive training in combined arms tactics. This meant the very officers in charge of deploying these tanks did not have experience or training to effectively deploy armored units alongside infantry. This same phenomenon, tanks advancing without infantry support, played out again and again during the Easter Offensive. The report goes on, citing intelligence gathered directly from PAVN personnel: "A training deficiency common to PAVN has been frequently cited in prisoner interrogation reports. No practical experience was provided in crew training for combined arms operations." Despite all of this, one section of the report stands out rather ominously: "As noted previously, the weakness and mistakes of the Offensive should not be expected on a continuing basis."[63] This would prove to be a prescient prediction in the spring of 1975 as PAVN armor rolled into Saigon.

The Easter Offensive of 1972 marked a significant departure from the previous tactics of PAVN. The Politburo's push for renewed general offensive in the South, as well as a large influx of Soviet tanks and other weaponry, gave the appearance of an unstoppable force bent on conquering Saigon, come hell or high water. Political considerations brought about by the Nixon administration's overtures to Moscow and Beijing provoked fears within North Vietnam's leadership that they would be betrayed once again by their communist patrons, despite assurances from Soviet and Chinese leadership as well as increased military and economic aid. North Vietnamese memories of Geneva 18 years prior led to increased paranoia and fears of abandonment in 1972. Therefore, the need for an immediate "go-for-broke"-style offensive was pushed to the fore due to increased geopolitical concerns.

However, the Politburo's insistence on an immediate offensive meant that PAVN's ranks were swelled with raw, inexperienced recruits. Recruits who likely had never even seen a tank before were given a brief four-month training session in the USSR before being thrown into the cauldron of battle. Other recruits were given little-to-no training driving their mothballed T-54s out of garages before facing US and ARVN forces. In short, an army that was new to the intrigues and difficulties of mechanized combined arms warfare was expected to win an outright victory against a technologically superior enemy.

ARVN soldiers parade a captured PAVN T-54 through the streets of Saigon in May 1972. (Wikimedia Commons/NARA)

Lastly, these tanks were placed under the command of officers who, while having combat experience in many instances, did not have any training in combined arms tactics. The initial shock of the Easter Offensive saw significant PAVN gains. However, as the offensive wore on, lack of training and experience among PAVN tank crews became apparent. What was meant to be an armored blitzkrieg devolved into an armored freeze. Despite the overwhelming presence of U.S. airpower, PAVN forces came close to breaking through at places like Quang Tri, Dong Ha, and An Loc. However, outnumbered and outgunned ARVN defenders were able to halt PAVN armored thrusts. While supply issues and U.S. airpower undoubtedly played roles in halting the offensive, these factors were secondary to the rushed nature of the Easter Offensive, poor PAVN command coordination, and the lack of training of the North Vietnamese.

CHAPTER 4

The Paris Peace Accords and the Fall of Saigon (1973–75)

The Paris Peace Accords[1]

The road to the 1973 Accords had begun in France's capital five years earlier. In May of 1968, as the embers of the Tet Offensive still burned, representatives of President Johnson's administration met with North Vietnamese officials to begin discussing political solutions for Southeast Asia. In what was largely an attempt to save a sinking Democratic Party from defeat in November,[2] Johnson sent Averill Harriman to Paris to determine on what issues the North Vietnamese would compromise if the United States were to propose a bombing halt. Facing Harriman was North Vietnamese negotiator Xuan Thuy, whose lack of political skill, Hanoi's Politburo calculated, would make substantive progress in these talks unlikely.

As predicted, the two camps descended into continuous rounds of recriminations and finger pointing.[3] Negotiating from a position of strength against a weakened administration, the North Vietnamese achieved several bombing halt concessions from Washington, with little concessions made by Hanoi. The Johnson peace talks came to a close as the White House came under the Republican control of Richard Nixon.[4] The failure of the Johnson peace overtures in the latter half of 1968 can also be partly attributed to the efforts of Anna Chennault. Chennault, the widow of the famous World War II "Flying Tigers" hero General Claire Chennault, was selected by Nixon to act as conduit between his campaign and the Saigon government. During the fall of 1968, Chennault (on Nixon's orders) began to convince the South Vietnamese to "hold on" and avoid accepting a

Johnson administration-led peace agreement. Chennault implied to South Vietnamese Ambassador Bui Diem that a better deal could be won for Saigon with Nixon in the White House. The plan worked. There was no lastminute October surprise in the form of a peace deal. Accordingly, Nixon won the 1968 election by a margin of 0.7 percent in the popular vote. The Chennault Affair (which remains a hotly contested anecdote of American politics to this day) achieved its aim by preventing the Democratic Party from winning the title of "peacemakers" before the 1968 election.[5]

President Richard Nixon took office in January 1969 with a plan to bring "an honorable end to the war in Vietnam."[6] Nixon and his national security advisor, Henry Kissinger, continued to negotiate with the North Vietnamese in Paris in the hopes that it would portray the strength of American resolve. However, the protests and political consternation surrounding Vietnam, as well as the war's stalemated nature, had for all intents and purposes forced the Nixon administration's hands. By 1970–71, both Nixon and Kissinger had accepted that a "decent interval" between the date of American withdrawal, the presidential election of 1972, and the likely fall of Saigon was the most realistic and politically attractive goal.[7] Larry Berman in his book, *No Peace, No Honor*, disputes the "decent-interval" theory by claiming that Nixon would have never accepted any sort of North Vietnamese victory in South Vietnam. However, more recent scholarship like that in Jeffrey Kimball's *Nixon's War in Vietnam* and Ken Hughes' *Fatal Politics* has argued the simple fact that continued talks and ultimate "success" in Paris would not have happened if Nixon and Kissinger did not openly pursue the "decent-interval" strategy with Hanoi. Additionally, as was noted in the last chapter, Nixon's desire to pursue détente overrode his concerns for continuing the war in Vietnam.[8] Accordingly, U.S. troop withdrawals continued despite concerns for South Vietnam's fighting capabilities. For example, following the disastrous South Vietnamese incursion into Laos in February 1971, Henry Kissinger cabled the U.S. ambassador to South Vietnam, Ellsworth Bunker, notifying him of the president's intention to immediately announce further U.S. troop withdrawals. In Kissinger's words, "I am sure you recognize that the withdrawal announcement contemplated by the President is a large one. However, it has become all the more necessary in view of the mixed results of the [Laos] operation and its unexpected conclusion which has placed the President under increasing political pressure here [in the United States]."[9]

After three years of negotiations, 1972 turned out to be the climactic year of the Paris peace talks. PAVN's Easter Offensive failed to topple the government of South Vietnamese President Nguyen Van Thieu. Thieu, who had won reelection the previous year in an unopposed field,[10] had been saved for the time being, giving Nixon and Kissinger an opportunity to make good on campaign promises for peace made in both 1968 and 1972. Nixon's overtures to both China and the Soviet Union also led to an opening where a peace agreement seemed possible.[11] However, South Vietnamese officials became angrier and angrier as the fall of 1972 wore on. A draft agreement of the Paris talks worked out between Kissinger and his North Vietnamese counterpart Le Duc Tho, for example, found its way into Thieu's hands by way of a captured Viet Cong political officer that October.[12] In a message to Henry Kissinger from Deputy Assistant for National Security Affairs Al Haig, Haig expressed that Thieu knew that he was being pressed into a corner by the agreement, knowing full well that either rejecting or accepting the agreement would spell doom for his government.[13]

Despite Thieu calling the agreement a "false peace," negotiations between Kissinger and Tho continued into December 1972. Despite a brief setback and subsequent return to hostilities in the form of the infamous "Christmas Bombings," the Paris Peace Accords went into effect in January 1973.[14] Despite last-minute pleading from President Van Thieu about the need to reach an agreement by which PAVN forces would be forced to depart South Vietnam,[15] over 150,000 PAVN troops remained in South Vietnam when both sides signed the accords on January 27, 1973.[16] Additionally, while the accords promised an end to hostilities in the South, an end to further infiltration of South Vietnam, and a full accounting for of MIA personnel, none of these provisions were ultimately adhered to.[17]

Fighting resumed shortly after the signing of the accords, with both the North and South Vietnamese blaming one another for breaking the agreement.[18] National reconciliation, free elections, and peaceful

Soviet Leader (and Khrushchev's successor) Leonid Brezhnev and U.S. President Richard Nixon talk through a translator during Brezhnev's June 1973 visit to the United States. (NARA/Wikimedia Commons)

reunification (all provisions within the Paris Peace Accords) were never implemented. For the North Vietnamese, the signing of the Paris Peace Accords was a great step forward, and in the words of PAVN General Van Tien Dung (who later commanded the victorious PAVN forces of 1975), the accords "opened up a new period in the South Vietnamese revolution: the period for completing the people's democratic revolution, and for reuniting the country."[19] Seeing a new opportunity opening as the final America forces withdrew in March 1973, North Vietnamese planners began to formulate a strategy for absolute victory.

North Vietnamese Preparations for the 1975 Offensive

While the ink on the Paris Peace Accords was still drying, Hanoi began to formulate plans for the continuation of its military struggle in the South.

In June 1973, the 21st Plenum of the Central Committee commenced in Hanoi. Le Duan, encouraged by the continued skirmishing in the South and by what he saw as South Vietnamese violations of the accords, gave an opening speech calling for another return to main-force warfare as a means of toppling the Saigon government. What differed in the current moment as opposed to 1972 was the presence of "leopard spot" formations of PAVN forces in the South.

As stated previously, a provision of the Paris Peace Accords allowed for over 150,000 PAVN troops to remain within South Vietnam and hold the positions that they had occupied since the opening days of the Easter Offensive. Subsequent maps of South Vietnam delineating PAVN troop positions had blotted spots dotted across the country, hence their nickname. In short, so long as they could be held, PAVN had incredibly effective jump-off points within South Vietnam itself for further offensive action. In July 1973, the Politburo approved Le Duan's plan for continued revolutionary violence in the South. Three months later, the strategy outlined at the 21st Plenum was formally approved.[20] As a sign of events to come, the 21st Plenum Resolution did not waver in its emphatic endorsement of a continued armed struggle:

> We must exploit the current favorable conditions in order to restore and develop a national people's economy suited toward our political responsibilities during the new phase, cause the Socialist North to make rapid progress on all fronts so that it constantly serves as the solid foundation and source of support for our revolutionary struggle aimed at achieving independence and democracy in South Vietnam.[21]

As part of the preparation for continued offensive action in the South, PAVN planners knew that they needed to rectify the tactical and strategic errors that emerged during the 1972 offensive. For General Giap, this was a critical problem that needed to be addressed before PAVN could be expected to take on and destroy large ARVN units. Specifically, the core tenets of combined arms operations, command and control, staff planning, and logistics, needed revamping before the upcoming struggle for South Vietnam. Realizing that only Moscow could provide such training, Hanoi sent Senior Colonel Nguyen Huu An (PAVN commander at the famous Ia Drang Valley battles of 1965) and a delegation of officers to the Soviet Union shortly after the conclusion of the 21st Plenum. The lessons learned in the Soviet Union in 1973 later played a huge role in the offensive of 1975.[22]

In March of 1974, after a year's worth of skirmishes and fighting with the South Vietnamese, Hanoi's Central Military Committee met to discuss the current situation in the South as well as future plans of action. From a logistical standpoint, the Ho Chi Minh Trail had reached the zenith of its logistical capability and efficiency. The absence of American airpower and the lack of any significant incursions since 1971 had allowed North Vietnamese engineers to turn the trail into major thoroughfare reliant on mechanized trucks and vehicles.

Additionally, a 1,000-mile pipeline was completed to link ever-precious fuel logistics between refineries in the North and PAVN forces in the South.[23] The rapid success in completing both the oil pipeline and the upgrades to the Ho Chi Minh Trail were major factors in the Central Military Committee's eventual decision to resume offensive operations in the South.[24] The March Conference, however, also noted some negative aspects of Hanoi's current position. Much of PAVN's heavy artillery and armor was in disrepair following the heavy fighting of 1972.[25] While Hanoi's patrons in Beijing and Moscow (who despite détente were still economically and militarily supplying Hanoi, albeit at diminished levels) pledged a combined $400 million in military aid during 1974, the North Vietnamese needed to be patient for the time being.[26] It is interesting to note, though, that both the PRC and Soviet Union began to wane in their unqualified support for North Vietnam during this time period. While aid still flowed to Hanoi, it was in reduced levels compared to years past (especially 1972).

In visits to Moscow and Beijing in 1973, Le Duan pleaded with Brezhnev and Mao to continue their increased levels of support. Both Moscow and Beijing refused. For Moscow, détente was not a diplomatic initiative worth jeopardizing. However, the Soviets did agree on a new economic and technical aid agreement and forgave part of Hanoi's war debt. The PRC, on the other hand, was much harsher in its rebuke. Following Le Duan's visit, the PRC told Hanoi to wait several years before launching a formal reunification campaign. This angered Le Duan and his compatriots immensely. In the words of historian Pierre Asselin, "Le Duan and other [North Vietnamese] leaders concluded, not incorrectly in retrospect, that Beijing preferred the Balkanization of Indochina, and the continued existence of two Vietnams" as a means of countering what Beijing saw as possible Soviet encroachment in Southeast Asia.[27]

In the words of General Dung, the North Vietnamese strategy for most of 1974 called for a buildup and preparation for 1975: "the goal was to raise the will to struggle, step up organizational discipline, and guarantee that all three kinds of troops [main-force troops, regional-force troops, and local guerilla militia] would victoriously complete every mission in the new period."[28] However, events in the United States in the late summer of 1974 gave Hanoi reason to be optimistic for its chances in 1975.

Since late 1973, the Watergate scandal had consumed the presidency of Richard Nixon. In previous years, Nixon had taken an incredibly hands-on, almost micro-managerial approach to the war in Vietnam. By 1974, Nixon left the conduct of the war to close advisors whose attachment to Vietnam paled in comparison to the president's.[29] Finally, amidst growing pressure from members of his own party, Nixon resigned the presidency. This led to Gerald Ford being sworn in.[30]

The North Vietnamese were elated at this news. In a Politburo Resolution released less than a week after Nixon's resignation, the North Vietnamese expressed the belief that Nixon's resignation once and for all "demonstrates the failure of America's world strategy." Furthermore, the document expresses an urgent need to step up combat operations in the South as a means of taking advantage of the chaos going on within the American political system.[31] The stage was set for renewed offensive action in the South aimed at testing both Saigon and Washington's reactions. This first test came at the end of 1974 in a place called Phuoc Long.

Phuoc Long and the Collapse of the Central Highlands

In May of 1974, a U.S. National Intelligence Estimate (NIE) was issued summarizing the likelihood of a major North Vietnamese invasion in 1974, as well as the increased capabilities of PAVN. The NIE stated that while a major offensive in 1974 was unlikely, it was increasingly probable that PAVN would shift back to "major warfare" in the near future. PAVN, by the spring of 1974, had replenished most of its stocks and was stronger than it was at the signing of the Paris Peace Accords in January 1973. Also of note in the NIE were the increased logistical capabilities of PAVN, as well as the implementation of "remedial training programs to overcome the shortcomings that emerged during the fighting of 1972." The NIE ended by saying that the current advantages in men, material, and logistics present within PAVN could enable it to move faster and more decisively than ever before. However, the NIE deemed a major PAVN offensive unlikely given Hanoi's uncertainty about American responses to such an action.[32]

Upon the resignation of Richard Nixon three months after the dissemination of the NIE, the North Vietnamese began to shift their own estimations. Hanoi found it increasingly unlikely that the politically hamstrung and economically preoccupied administration of President Ford would become re-entangled in Vietnam.[33] However, the North Vietnamese were still hesitant to launch a massive "go for broke"-style offensive in the South.

In December 1974, PAVN General Tran Van Tra presented a plan to attack Phuoc Long province in MR-3 (just south of the Central Highlands) and seize the vital road junction on Dong Xoai. Despite pushback from PAVN General Staff and (initially) Le Duan, Tra's plan was approved. In part, the attack on Phuoc Long was approved as a means of testing whether the Ford administration would react aggressively to renewed PAVN offensive action.

On December 13, 1974, Tra's forces launched their attack into Phuoc Long. PAVN forces swept in and quickly captured the road junction town of Bu Dang on December 14. PAVN then began to advance quickly down Route 14, thus tightening the noose around Dong Xoai. The attacks in Phuoc Long showed several improvements in PAVN's use of armor. For example, at the battles for Ba Ra Mountain and Phuoc Binh, PAVN commanders effectively deployed infantry alongside armor. Recognizing both terrain difficulties as well as the tanks' vulnerabilities, infantry was deployed in close cohesion with PAVN T-54/55 tanks. PAVN sappers often rode on top of T-55 tanks to provide immediate infantry support when needed. Additionally, PAVN had learned from their experiences in 1972 dealing with M72 LAW rockets and had welded heavier armor to the more vulnerable parts of their T-55s.[34]

The attack on Phuoc Long proved to be a resounding success when, on January 6, 1975, T-54 tanks advanced on and captured the provincial headquarters. President Ford, faced with a lack of public support as well as congressional resolutions which hindered his ability to retaliate, was reduced to ordering the USS *Enterprise* to divert toward Vietnam as a show of force.[35] The North Vietnamese were elated by the lack of a U.S. response, and took it as a sign that continued offensive action, this time in the very near future, was the best course of action. In the words of General Dung, "the enemy's weakness was a signal that a new opportunity was on the way.... The situation now had infinite possibilities for us."[36]

Shortly after the fall of Phuoc Long, PAVN planners met once again to discuss continued offensive actions aimed at keeping the pressure on the Saigon government. On January 9, 1975, secretary of the North Vietnamese Central Military Committee General Vo Nguyen Giap approved a plan called "Campaign 275." Campaign 275 called for an attack directly into the Central Highlands of South Vietnam, with the main objective of capturing the provincial capital of Ban Me Thout. If all went according to plan, this initial thrust of campaign 275 would cut South Vietnam in half, paving the way to Saigon.[37]

On March 4, 1975, the attack into the Central Highlands began. Instead of attacking Ban Me Thout head-on, PAVN sought to surround and isolate it first.[38] In a further shift away from the failed strategies of 1972, PAVN deployed its forces in large numbers in coordinated attacks aimed at the same objective.[39] Fighting in and around Ban Me Thout continued for almost two weeks. PAVN, particularly parts of its armored forces, began to display the same kinds of command-and-control issues that had plagued its units in 1972. For example, on March 8, PAVN infantry units attacking nearby ARVN firebases got lost and fell prey to concentrated artillery fire. They experienced further issues when a PAVN armored assault on March 14 descended into chaos after one tank smashed its main gun by driving into a tree, while another drove into a ditch. However, on March 16, PAVN successfully captured Ban Me Thout, sending South Vietnamese forces into disarray.[40]

What happened following the fall of Ban Me Thout sealed the fate of South Vietnam. After a secret emergency meeting with his National Security Council on March 14, South Vietnamese President Nguyen Van Thieu determined that the Central Highlands were lost. In order to salvage what ARVN forces were left, President Thieu ordered a withdrawal out of the Central Highlands and a redeployment to South Vietnam's coastal lowlands. However, according to one observer, "The withdrawal lacked unity and control right from the moment it first started."[41] Only three days' worth of planning preceded the withdrawal. Because of the quick turnaround and sudden orders, ARVN forces were unable to effectively coordinate counterattacks, blocking positions, and delaying actions, let alone move several ARVN divisions with PAVN hot on their heels.[42]

A memo from the consul general in Nha Trang to Ambassador Graham Martin in Saigon noted that news broadcasts of President Thieu's order set off widespread panic throughout the Central Highlands. Refugees from Pleiku and Ban Me Thout intermingled with retreating ARVN forces to create a massive horde that clogged up roadways. PAVN forces, initially caught off guard by such a drastic maneuver, quickly reassembled and advanced on the retreating column. By the time the column reached the coast on March 23, the original ARVN force of 200,000 men was now a mere 60,000. Untold numbers of refugees also perished in the panicked withdrawal.[43]

In light of the panicked withdrawal, General Giap urgently cabled General Dung exclaiming, "In view of this situation, the Politburo's resolve is, as has already been transmitted to you, to move as fast as possible, acting with daring and surprise (in terms of direction, of forces, and of timing) to defeat the enemy's plan and quickly achieve our strategic goal."[44] In the last week of March 1975, PAVN moved rapidly on South Vietnam's northernmost coastal cities. From March 21–25, PAVN advanced on and subsequently captured the old Imperial capital of Hue, nearly destroying the ARVN 1st Infantry Division. On March 29, amid the chaos of the city's ports where refugees and ARVN soldiers alike attempted climb aboard boats to escape the oncoming communists, PAVN captured the vital city of Da Nang.[45] On March 28, Henry Kissinger told a beleaguered and embittered President Ford, "I don't think South Vietnam can make it.... It is a moral collapse of the United States."[46]

The Fall of Saigon and Hanoi's Image of Victory

Following the tumultuous events of late March, Hanoi smelled blood in the water. The disastrous withdrawal of ARVN forces from the Central Highlands, the subsequent capture of the coastal cities of Hue and Da Nang, and the continued lack of American response to the unfolding events gave Hanoi the green light to go for a coup de grâce against Saigon. In one of the last great gasps of the ARVN, from April 9–20 the town of Xuan Loc 37 miles northeast of Saigon held out against all odds. In the last successful ARVN helicopter lift of the war, an ARVN airborne brigade was flown in to help relieve the threatened garrison of General Le Minh Dao. Despite heroic ARVN feats, PAVN artillery eventually broke the defense of Xuan Loc and the city fell in what author Max Hastings called "a shining memory [for South Vietnam], in the midst of a grand narrative of humiliation."[47]

Meanwhile, 200 miles east of Saigon, the coastal city of Phan Rang was quickly falling to PAVN armor. On April 16, a PAVN armored attack, closely coordinated with infantry, overwhelmed ARVN defenses within a matter of hours. Fleeing ARVN troops desperately tried to get aboard ships headed out into the South China Sea, only to be met with point-blank tank fire from PAVN T-54/55s that had advanced all the way to Phan Rang's harbor facilities. Two days later and 90 miles down the coastal road at the city of Phan Thiet, a PAVN armored unit adhering to "standard Soviet armor doctrine" overran the city in five hours.[48]

On the morning of April 21, 1975, as the communist noose began to tighten around Saigon, South Vietnamese President Nguyen Van Thieu resigned the presidency and was replaced by his vice president, Tran Van Huong.[49] Upon receiving news of Thieu's resignation, Hanoi sent a cable out to its forces surrounding Saigon urging them to "quickly and urgently military [sic] carry out attack plans with absolute determination and resolve, annihilate truly large numbers of enemy troops, and seize and occupy the designated targets."[50] On April 23, in a speech at Tulane University President Ford declared "the war in Vietnam is over as far as the United States is concerned."[51] Two days later, the former president Thieu and his former prime minister General Tran Thien Khiem were evacuated via U.S. helicopters out of Vietnam. On April 27, PAVN rockets began to land in Saigon as PAVN armored units cut the last remaining road that linked South Vietnam's capital city to the sea. Two days later, heavy bombardments of Saigon's airport as well as the capture of Cu Chi 25 miles from the capital city confirmed the fate of the Republic of Vietnam.

On April 30 at 1015, General Duong Van Minh (who had since taken over for Huong) announced South Vietnam's surrender.[52] Just before dawn on May 1, Colonel Bui Tin, a North Vietnamese journalist, hitched a ride on top of one of three PAVN T-54s that was leading the victorious march into Saigon. Being in possession of a photograph of the presidential palace, Bui Tin guided the T-54 and its crew to the symbolic center of the South Vietnamese state. Because the fighting had ceased following the surrender announcement, the only damage done to the presidential palace that day was caused when Bui Tin's T-54 crashed through the palace's iron gate.[53] For the North Vietnamese, Vietnam was now unified. Furthermore, the lasting image of this momentous victory almost 30 years in the making was the appearance of a Soviet-made T-54 tank, brandishing a Viet Cong flag crashing through the gates of the "puppet regime's" presidential palace. Victory had been won under the treads of a tank.

From the capitulation of the French garrison at Dien Bien Phu in 1954 to the fall of Saigon in 1975, Vietnamese communist political and military forces sought to navigate increasingly troubled waters within the global communist camp. For almost the entirety of the war against the French, Ho Chi Minh and the Viet Minh relied on the newly christened PRC for military and political support. The PRC played a major role in advising Viet Minh forces through its CMAG delegations, and helped the Vietnamese communists successfully employ hard-won lessons from the Chinese Civil War. Had it not been for the PRC and CMAG, the decisive deployment of Viet Minh artillery at Dien Bien Phu might not have happened.

While the Soviet Union vocally supported Ho's struggle against the French, Josef Stalin expressed only a fleeting interest toward events in Southeast Asia. Following the Viet Minh victory at Dien Bien Phu, Ho Chi Minh and his compatriots expected to win major concessions at the Geneva Conference of 1954. However, both the PRC and Soviet Union had pressured Ho to accept much more conciliatory terms by the time the Geneva Conference came to a close in July 1954. Concerns over Europe as well as a possible U.S. intervention in Indochina overrode the wishes of the Viet Minh. The bitter partition of Vietnam into a communist North and a non-communist South not only prolonged Hanoi's struggle for unification, but it instilled a permanent skepticism toward Beijing and Moscow. Hanoi, for the rest of its struggle, was fearful that its benefactors in Beijing and Moscow would sacrifice the interests of Vietnam for their own geopolitical benefits.

In 1956, events in Poland and Hungary rocked the communist world. Additionally, the death of Josef Stalin two years earlier left the mantle of "leadership" in the communist world up for grabs. Stalin's successor Nikita Khrushchev sought to de-Stalinize the Soviet Union and its allies, much to the chagrin of PRC leader Mao Zedong. The Soviet reaction to Hungary and Poland, as well as its perceived chauvinistic attitude towards the PRC, led to an ever-widening split between Beijing and Moscow. Accordingly, Hanoi was forced to carefully balance its political and military strategies going forward. By 1959, Hanoi determined that the provisions of the Geneva Accords would not be adhered to, thus necessitating a renewed military struggle. Hanoi's 15th Plenum of 1959 not only called for increased aggressive military struggle in the South, but it also solidified the ascension of Le Duan. Ho Chi Minh, whose political record suffered greatly after the doomed land reform campaigns of 1956, was swept aside by a much more aggressive faction within the North Vietnamese Politburo. This faction, while still leaning towards the PRC, refused to publicly denounce Moscow, thus maintaining the careful diplomatic balance amidst the Sino-Soviet split.

Despite adopting a Vietnamized version of Mao's people's war, Hanoi's struggle for Southern liberation did not completely shun the idea of larger, more mechanized forms of warfare. This was reflected by the formation of PAVN's nascent armored forces in 1959. After receiving Soviet-made tanks and training limited numbers of tank crews, Hanoi began to prepare for a possible large-scale conventional war in the South. While Khrushchev's policy of "peaceful coexistence" with the West was anathema to Hanoi's strategy, the North Vietnamese refused to shun Moscow, especially when it came to military technology.

The assassination of RVN President Ngo Dinh Diem and the Gulf of Tonkin incident a year later greatly shifted the path of the Vietnam War. After the assassination of Diem, Hanoi decided to escalate the war in the South by sending even greater numbers of troops and supplies down the Ho Chi Minh trail. When the United States escalated its efforts following the Gulf of Tonkin, Moscow began to slowly recalculate its approach to Vietnam. This was especially true after the ouster of Khrushchev and the subsequent rise of Leonid Brezhnev. The Soviet Union henceforth did not play an idle role in Southeast Asia. Rather, Moscow would steadily ratchet up its support for Vietnam, much to the chagrin of the PRC.

As the war escalated, Hanoi determined that it needed to pursue bigger battles and larger engagements that were contrary to the Maoist people's war approach. In order to achieve success in these battles against American forces, Hanoi began to rely more heavily on increasingly advanced military technology that Moscow could supply and Beijing could not. Additionally, the excesses of Mao's Cultural Revolution contributed to the already ongoing souring of Sino-Vietnamese relations. The Tet Offensive of 1968 marked a major shift in PAVN strategy that almost completely ignored the tenets of the people's war strategy. Additionally, the attack at Lang Vei illustrated a greater reliance on Soviet technology, more specifically with the use of tanks in an offensive role.

As U.S. troops began to withdraw from Vietnam in 1969, a greater emphasis was placed on the South Vietnamese taking up larger combat roles in their fight against PAVN and VC. However, Operation *Lam Son 719* in 1971 illustrated not only ARVN's continued inability to fight on alone, but it also showed a massive increase in PAVN's weapons capabilities. The successful use of armor in 1968 and 1971 led PAVN to lean even harder into conventional, mechanized military tactics. This inevitably led to the Easter Offensive of 1972. Faced with increased international pressures in the form of Nixon's overtures to Beijing and Moscow, Hanoi feared a repeat of Geneva in 1954. Therefore, the Easter Offensive was launched on March 30, 1972, with massed armor formations. However, the lack of proper combined arms training prior to the offensive severely hindered the ability of PAVN tank crews to conduct proper offensive operations. This led to a less than stellar performance of PAVN forces and enabled the Saigon government of President Thieu to survive another day.

The Paris Peace Accords gave Hanoi another chance to rectify its strategic errors from years past. In addition to forcing the Americans out of Southeast Asia, the accords allowed PAVN to keep a substantial number of its forces within South Vietnam. Despite Beijing and Moscow's lessened support for Hanoi in light of détente, the North Vietnamese continued to put pressure on Saigon in 1973–74. The formal adoption of plans for reunification and the political consternation in the United States gave Hanoi the opportunity to move forward with its strategic goals. Lessons learned and revisited from its experience in 1972 led PAVN to drastically improve its logistical and strategic capabilities. The attack on Phuoc Long and the subsequent fall of the Central Highlands during January–April 1975 illustrated the improved nature of PAVN armored forces. While far from perfect, PAVN armor performance in 1975 reflected a much more measured and coordinated approach to combined arms warfare. The lasting image of April 1975 for Hanoi was the image of a Soviet-made T-54 tank smashing through the gates of Saigon. The red banner flying over the French Barracks at Dien Bien Phu in 1954 had been replaced with 40 tons of steel breaking through a metal gate in 1975.

PAVN's progression from a light infantry force fighting in rural areas to a largely mechanized force driving tanks into urban areas followed a steady flow of events that reflected the geopolitics Hanoi found itself mired in. While the PRC played an instrumental role in forming and training the units of the Viet Minh that eventually became PAVN, Hanoi never fully adopted Mao's war strategies. While the idea of a people's war played a vital role in informing Hanoi's early strategies, it was never fully adopted, and was eventually subsumed by more ambitious forms of

[Above and opposite] Tank 843 sits today in front of what once was the South Vietnamese presidential palace. The building has been converted to a museum and is now called the Independence Palace. (Author photo)

military strategy. American escalation of the war in Vietnam—as well as increased Soviet support—led Hanoi to rely more exclusively on heavy weaponry and advanced military technology, neither of which Beijing could provide in great numbers.

Additionally, the PRC became increasingly chauvinistic and demanding towards Hanoi as the Sino-Soviet split worsened and Mao's Cultural Revolution accelerated. This, combined with the desire to deploy heavy weaponry, led Hanoi to rely more and more on the support of Moscow.

Soviet support perhaps is best embodied by the increasing use of tanks starting (albeit in a limited manner) in 1968 and becoming ubiquitous in 1975. The tank attack at Lang Vei in 1968, Sergeant Luom's brave stance at Dong Ha in 1972, and the crashing of the presidential palace gates in 1975 did not happen in a vacuum. Rather, the geopolitics of the communist world and the added pressures of U.S. escalation forced Hanoi to adopt new strategies, new tactics, and new technologies revolving around armored forces. Today, PAVN T-54 Tank 843 still sits on the grounds of what was once the South Vietnamese presidential palace.[54] Tank 843 stands as a monument both to Hanoi's victory and its military evolution from 1954–75.

EPILOGUE

From War, to Peace, to War Once Again (1975–91)

As PAVN tanks crashed into Saigon's presidential palace on April 30, 1975, it appeared that the now-unified nation of Vietnam would finally experience a lasting peace. However, once again, pressures brought on by both Beijing and Moscow made this endeavor difficult to achieve. Shortly after the fall of Saigon, Hanoi began to reach out to its patrons in the Soviet Union and the PRC for economic assistance to help rebuild its newly unified nation. The PRC continued to worry about the ever-growing relationship between Moscow and Hanoi. In July 1975, the PRC warned Hanoi that continued friendly relations with the "hegemonist [*sic*]" Soviet Union would further hamper Sino-Vietnamese relations.[1] Zhou Enlai, in a meeting with Vietnamese representatives on August 15, 1975, rebuffed requests for post-war reconstruction by claiming that the spoils of war left behind by the now defunct Saigon regime would be adequate for Hanoi.

To add insult to injury, that same year, the PRC pledged $1 billion towards the assistance of the newly victorious Khmer Rouge regime in Cambodia. The final nail in the coffin of Sino-Vietnamese friendship and goodwill was hammered home in September 1975. During a meeting with Le Duan in Beijing, Mao personally rebuffed and refused future economic support for Vietnam.[2] During the meeting, Mao emphatically said "today, you are not the poorest under heaven. We are the poorest. We have a population of 800 million. Our leadership is now facing a crisis. The Premier (Zhou) is not in good health, he had four operations in one year and [the situation] is dangerous.... I am 82 years old. I am very ill. [Mao points to Deng Xiaoping.] Only he is young and strong."[3]

Deng Xiaoping's Ascension to PRC Leadership (1975–78)

Indeed, China was convulsing with political upheaval. Still reeling from the ravages wrought by the Cultural Revolution, the PRC found itself at a crossroads in 1975. As mentioned by Mao to Le Duan in September, both he and Zhou Enlai (the two most well-known and powerful leaders in the country) were gravely ill. Within the CCP, power struggles continued. While Hua Guofeng, a younger party leader, was considered the heir apparent to Mao, a recently rehabilitated Deng Xiaoping had begun to exert more and more influence within the CCP. Simultaneously, Mao's wife, Jiang Qing, and three other prominent party zealots—Wang Hongwen, Zhang Chunqiao, and Yao Wenyuan, collectively referred to as the Gang of Four,—began to agitate for a return to radical politics.[4] With Zhou Enlai still in hospital, it seemed that any moderating influence that could have kept the Gang of Four on a tight leash was incapacitated. Jiang began to direct her ire towards Deng, whose "empiricism" (arguments in favor of economic reform and modernization) was viewed as a counterrevolutionary threat.[5]

Political maneuvering continued between the Gang of Four and Deng Xiaoping for almost two years. However, on September 9, 1976, a tectonic shift occurred in the CCP and Chinese society. Mao Zedong, the revolutionary icon and god-like leader of the People's Republic of China, died from health complications related to "undiagnosed Lou Gehrig's Disease."[6] With Mao gone, Jiang and the Gang of Four had lost their political cover. A month after Mao's death, rallies in Beijing and Shanghai saw masses of people denouncing the Gang of Four. Jiang and her clique represented the embodiment of the Cultural Revolution's excesses. The demonstrations sentenced the Gang of Four to political irrelevance, while Hua Guofeng ascended as chairman of the CCP.[7]

However, less than a year after Mao's death, Hua's grasp on CCP decision-making was challenged by the perpetually embattled Deng Xiaoping. In 1977, the PRC under Hua's leadership still failed to meet industrial production targets. Workers went on strike. An economic crisis loomed. CCP leadership encouraged Hua to bring the once again ostracized Deng Xiaoping out of isolation. Hua complied and in July

1977, Deng was present within the CCP Central Committee. Deng's uncanny record of political survivability remained intact due to his unique bureaucratic skills and ability to influence those around him.[8] Deng reemerged in the summer of 1977 and became the CCP vice chairman, vice chairman of the Central Military Committee, deputy premier, and chief of the People's Liberation Army (PLA) General Staff. For the next year and a half, Deng continued to wage a political war with Hua. This culminated in November 1978 at the Third Plenum of the Eleventh CCP Congress when, after several blistering speeches blaming Hua and his allies for the continuing the ruinous policies of the Cultural Revolution, Deng "gradually became the preeminent decision-maker in China."[9] As China began to politically re-align itself, so too did its neighbor and former ally.

Vietnam, the Soviet Union, and the "Treaty of Friendship and Cooperation"

Victory in Saigon did not immediately bring about a stable and secure Vietnam. Faced with a war-torn country and a former benefactor's continued repudiation, Hanoi once again looked towards Moscow for help. On November 1, 1978, a Vietnamese delegation led by Le Duan and Pham Van Dong arrived in Moscow. Two days later, the Soviets and Vietnamese signed the "Treaty of Friendship and Cooperation." The treaty, on a macro level, was summed up by Article 4: "The two parties shall do their utmost to consolidate the world socialist system and actively contribute to the development and defense of the socialist gains." However, Article 6 of the treaty contained the most consequential passage:

> In case either party is attacked or threatened with attack, the two parties signatory to the treaty shall immediately consult each other with a view to eliminating the threat, and shall take appropriate and effective measures to safeguard peace and the security of the two countries.[10]

Reading Article 6, a specific word stands out: "consult." Rather than a definitive security guarantee that would necessitate that Moscow would intervene if Vietnam was attacked (and vice versa), Article 6 merely stated that the signatory would talk things out in the event of a military crisis.

One wonders why such a feckless treaty was signed by Hanoi. Political Scientist Stephen J. Morris claims that Hanoi viewed the treaty "as a minimal insurance policy" that would hopefully provide "a protective shield for Vietnam." Especially considering that Vietnam's leadership had already set in motion plans to attack its intransigent and radicalized neighbor: Cambodia.[11]

The PRC under Deng Xiaoping had already begun to dramatically expand Beijing's support for the increasingly genocidal regime in Cambodia.[12] Deng, unlike previous PRC figures such as Zhou Enlai, had no personal connection with Hanoi and therefore had little patience when it came to perceived slights or transgressions emanating from Hanoi.[13] Deng viewed the 1978 treaty as a very significant transgression that repudiated the PRC's previous advice to Hanoi. In April 1975, just prior to the fall of Saigon, Le Duan had visited Beijing and spoken with none other than Deng himself. During the meeting, Deng encouraged Le Duan to enter into an anti-Soviet coalition with Beijing. Deng explained to Le Duan that previous cracks in Sino-Vietnamese relations were the fault of Ho Chi Minh and could now be rectified, especially considering what the PRC saw as a looming Soviet threat to Asian communist movements. Le Duan rejected both assertions and left Beijing with great haste. No joint communique (a typical custom of diplomatic conferences) was issued.[14] Not only did Deng lack any personal rapport with the Vietnamese, but his only significant exchange with Le Duan prior to his ascension to power had been an abysmal failure.

The Vietnamese-Cambodian Struggle (1970–79)

The Khmer Rouge in Cambodia continued to pursue a maniacal "Year Zero" campaign against its own population. Shortly after the Khmer Rouge victory in April 1975, the major cities of Cambodia were emptied, and their residents were forced into rural communes. Former officials and military officers of the ousted Lon Nol government were executed outright. The Khmer Rouge pursued a "hyperMaoist [sic]" model that combined elements of the Cultural Revolution and Great Leap Forward, except at a much more rapid pace and in an even more radical manner. One Khmer Rouge Party memo exclaimed, "Our socialism is characterized by its speed.... Compared to other countries, in terms of method we are extremely fast."[15]

Cambodia under the Khmer Rogue became known (rather ironically) as "Democratic Kampuchea" (DK). The recently exiled city dwellers became an enslaved agricultural army intended to be the vanguard of a "worker-peasant" revolution.[16] In the words of historian Robert Service, the Khmer Rouge "was unique in the Marxist tradition for treating urban life not as a prerequisite of communist progress but as an iniquity to be eliminated."[17] For Pol Pot, the leader of the Khmer Rouge and DK, emptying the cities and forcing former urbanites into the countryside was also a way of exerting continued control over a population that he still did not trust. Khmer Rouge leaders viewed city dwellers as a hostile demographic that left Cambodia vulnerable to subversion. Additionally, the presence of ethnic minorities within the cities (particularly ethnic Vietnamese) was considered a potential fifth column by Pol Pot and his chief cadres.[18]

The presence of xenophobia in Cambodian attitudes towards the Vietnamese dates back for centuries to when the Champa and Khmer kingdoms (of present-day Cambodia) warred with their Vietnamese neighbors over control of Indochina. This culminated in the 19th century, when Vietnamese dynastic rulers turned the neighboring kingdom of Cambodia into a protectorate and began to impose Vietnamese culture upon the Cambodians. As Stephen Morris explains, "the cultural arrogance" meted out by the Vietnamese upon the Cambodians made them "hereditary enemies in the eyes of Cambodians until the present day."[19] Thus, despite being nominal allies during the three decades of fighting in Indochina, Cambodian communists and Vietnamese communists maintained strained relations due to their long national histories.

For example, during the Khmer Rouge's early struggles against the Cambodian government, Hanoi refused to give weaponry and supplies to the Khmer Rouge, which caused Pol Pot and his allies to feel a sense of abandonment. Hanoi viewed the Cambodian state in the mid- to late 1960s (then under the rule of Norodom Sihanouk) as a tacit ally because Phnom Penh allowed PAVN and VC forces to use Cambodian border areas as staging points and sanctuaries during their struggle against U.S. and ARVN forces. Additionally, Hanoi viewed the Khmer Rouge as a ragtag force that was incapable of establishing itself as a legitimate opponent to Phnom Penh.[20]

However, this coldness changed in April 1970 when Sihanouk was overthrown by his own prime minister, Lon Nol, in a coup. Faced with a newly installed hostile regime in Phnom Penh, Hanoi had no choice but to decisively side with Pol Pot and the Khmer Rouge as a means of keeping PAVN/VC supply lines and sanctuaries open.[21] However, the Khmer Rouge did not wholly acquiesce to this new arrangement. For starters, the anti-Lon Nol coalition now present in Cambodia (dubbed the National United Front of Cambodia, or FUNK) contained a multitude of factions with various allegiances and goals. There were Sihanouk loyalists who sought to return the prince to his throne, and the Khmer Viet Minh who were aligned with Hanoi and sought to foster closer ties with their Vietnamese counterparts. Lastly, there was the Khmer Rouge, which was much more nationalistic and Maoist than its counterparts. Accordingly, the Khmer Rouge began cleansing the FUNK's ranks of pro-Hanoi cadres as early as 1972.[22] It was also in 1972 when, due to the launching of the Easter Offensive, many of the remaining PAVN/VC main force units left their staging areas in Cambodia to participate in the attacks on South Vietnam. This led to a power vacuum which the Khmer Rouge almost immediately filled. By 1975, the Khmer Rouge's triumph in Cambodia (both over the Lon Nol government as well as the other resistance factions) was a fait accompli.[23]

The project previously labelled as "hyperMaoist [sic]" reached even more horrific heights in the years immediately following the fall of Phnom Penh. After its victory, the Khmer Rouge expelled some 150,000 ethnic Vietnamese residing in Cambodia. In the next two years, some 10–20,000 ethnic Vietnamese remaining in Cambodia were hunted down and killed. In a 1978 speech to the Khmer Rouge (more formally called the Communist Party of Kampuchea, or CPK), Pol Pot called for his fellow cadres to "firmly stir up national hatred and class hatred for the aggressive Vietnamese enemy, in order to turn this hatred into material hatred."[24]

Other ethnic minorities such as the Cham and ethnic Chinese residing in Cambodia also suffered greatly under the Khmer Rouge. For the Chams, their religion (they were predominantly Islamic) singled them out as potential threats to Cambodia. For the Chinese, their reputation as a merchant class singled them out as a bourgeois threat.[25] In both cases, both the Chams and Chinese suffered greatly. For example, of the 400,000 ethnic Chinese residing in Cambodia in 1975, only 215,000 remained alive by 1979.[26]

For the rest of those living under the rule of the Khmer Rouge, Pol Pot's agrarian revolution began to deteriorate, and by 1977 famine started to set in. In some districts, 70 percent of the population withered away and perished. Those who voiced concern over rations in Khmer Rouge communes or those who were caught stealing food to feed their children were immediately executed.[27] Food was used as a weapon. Upon hearing that some families were scrounging for mice, insects, and rotting fruit to eat, Pol Pot made it a capital offense to pick up fallen coconuts.[28] All told, the Khmer Rouge would kill over 1.5 million people during its nightmarish rule over Cambodia.[29]

As millions of Cambodians began to perish in what would become known as the "killing fields," Khmer Rouge forces began to raid villages just across the border in Vietnam. For the Khmer Rouge, the Mekong delta in Vietnam (called "Kampuchea Krom" by Cambodians) was rightfully part of Cambodia and belonged as part of a (now-) unified Cambodian state. Attacks against Vietnam started in the spring of 1977. On September 24, 1977, Khmer Rouge forces launched a massive cross-border attack into Vietnam's Tay Ninh province. The Khmer Rouge proceeded to massacre over 300 Vietnamese civilians and Cambodian refugees indiscriminately. Taken by surprise, it took PAVN forces a week to push out the Khmer Rouge.

Less than a month after the massacres in Tay Ninh, Pol Pot visited Beijing. On October 5, the CCP Ministry of Defense signed a protocol pledging arms deliveries to Phnom Penh. Despite the horrors that the Khmer Rouge was committing against ethnic Chinese in Cambodia, Beijing viewed Cambodia as a valuable chess piece in the geopolitical struggle unfolding in Cambodia. In the words of Chinese Foreign Minister

Huang Hua, "We support the stand of Cambodia and her people against Soviet revisionist social-imperialism and will not watch indifferently."[30]

On December 31, Phnom Penh severed diplomatic ties with Hanoi.[31] On April 24, 1978, two Khmer Rouge divisions attacked the Vietnamese village of Ba Chuc. After penetrating nearly 2 kilometers into Vietnam, the Khmer Rouge began to systematically slaughter 2,000 Vietnamese civilians.[32] By May 1978, regular fighting was occurring on both sides of the Vietnamese-Cambodian border, with Vietnamese fighter bombers carrying out daily missions.[33] On May 10, a Khmer Rouge radio station (echoing a previous directive from Pol Pot) pushed its listeners to kill 30 Vietnamese for every dead Cambodian. The polemic continued in a rather cynical mathematical equation: "Only 2 million troops to crush the 50 million Vietnamese, and we would still have 6 million people left."[34] In two years of cross-border raids into Vietnam, the Khmer Rouge had killed 30,000 Vietnamese soldiers and civilians.[35] Needless to say, Hanoi was not going to let this go unanswered.

With the increased border clashes and continued political pressure with Beijing, Hanoi also began to delve into xenophobic paranoia. Hanoi had watched as relations between Phnom Penh and Beijing strengthened since the fall of Saigon in 1975. As the border clashes of 1977–78 intensified, Hanoi began to protest Beijing's lack of concern and, at times, outright apathy to the fighting. In January 1978, the Vietnamese ambassador to Beijing registered his "dissatisfaction" with CCP media and its bias towards the Khmer Rouge's viewpoint of the border clashes.[36] The following month, Vietnamese media began to assert that Khmer Rouge forces were acting on behalf of the "imperialists and international reactionaries." While "imperialists" was clearly a swipe at the United States, "international reactionaries" was a thinly veiled polemic against Beijing. The full transcript lays it out clearly:

> Assisted and encouraged by the imperialists and international reactionaries, the Kampuchean [Cambodian] authorities have turned friends into foes and pointed their guns at their old comrades-in-arms who helped them win victory.... Those who have used Kampuchea to attack Vietnam have also made a wrong move and committed a blunder in the choice of allies and objectives.[37]

The clear insinuation in the above quote is that the PRC was encouraging the Khmer Rouge to attack Vietnam. In conversations with Soviet officials, the Vietnamese were even more blunt. In a conversation with a Soviet diplomat, Vietnamese Politburo Central Committee Member Tran Quyen insisted that the border clashes were being spurred on by Beijing as a means of keeping Vietnam from achieving post-war socialist reconstruction. The Soviet Union joined in on the accusations by claiming Beijing was purposefully provoking the deteriorating relations between Cambodia and Vietnam. Beijing hit back, saying that all of this was an attempt by the Soviet Union to pursue regime change in Cambodia, thus helping Moscow achieve "its strategic aim of establishing domination over Southeast Asia."[38]

As tensions increased, the Soviets began to firmly back Hanoi in the burgeoning crisis. Several months prior to the Treaty of Friendship in the summer of 1978, the Soviets had begun to supply large quantities of military aid to Hanoi for the first time since the fall of Saigon.[39] In June 1978, as fighting continued along the Cambodian-Vietnamese border, Le Duan left Hanoi with a delegation for Moscow. While the minutes of these Moscow meetings remain unrecorded, it is likely that this was an attempt by the Vietnamese to gauge whether Moscow would acquiesce to a Vietnamese invasion of Cambodia.[40]

That same month, the Vietnamese Politburo met in Hanoi. Here, major decisions were made regarding the future of Vietnamese foreign policy in Southeast Asia. First, in a shocking testament to the new geopolitical stance off Hanoi, China was declared as Vietnam's foremost political adversary. To the Politburo in 1978, Beijing had replaced the United States as the foremost meddler in Southeast Asian affairs. Building on this, the Politburo labeled the Khmer Rouge as Beijing's proxy. Lastly, and accordingly, the Politburo called for a military invasion of Cambodia to dislodge the Khmer Rouge.[41] In November, with the Treaty of Friendship signed between Moscow and Hanoi, the Vietnamese began to move forward with their invasion plans.

Starting in mid-November, two PAVN infantry divisions began to move into Cambodia in a probing manner towards the town of Kratie. A month later on Christmas Day 1978, Vietnam launched a full-scale invasion of Cambodia, capturing Kratie within five days. The capture of this vital transportation junction enabled Vietnamese forces to perform a pincer move south and cut off large numbers of Khmer Rouge forces.[42] In what one observer called "a blitzkrieg attack on Cambodia,"[43] Vietnamese forces cut off Cambodian strongholds and raced towards the capital of Phnom Penh. For two weeks, PAVN forces advanced nearly 75 kilometers per day.[44] Finally on January 7, 1979, the Khmer Rouge was ousted from power in Phnom Penh and was replaced by a Vietnamese-friendly government under Heng Samrin.[45]

The Third Indochina War and the Emergence of a New Asia (1979–91)

Over the several years leading up to the Vietnamese invasion of Cambodia, the PRC's relationship with Hanoi transformed from that of strain to that of downright hostility. From 1974–78, there had been an annual increase in border incidents between China and Vietnam. One such incident on May 4, 1977, saw 500 PAVN troops harass and beat Chinese rail workers near the ironically named "Friendship Pass" border crossing. In 1974, there were 179 recorded border incidents. By 1978, there were 812. Additionally, the issue of the Paracel Islands continued to be a sticking point. These islands in the middle of the South China Sea were seized by the Chinese in January 1974, much to the chagrin of Hanoi. Now that tensions along the Vietnamese-Cambodian border were coming to a head, Hanoi began to raise territorial issues with its northern neighbor as well.

In 1977, Hanoi signed a "Treaty of Friendship and Cooperation" with Laos. Beijing, predictably, saw this as an attempt at "regional hegemony" on the part of Vietnam.[46] Additionally, Vietnam's mistreatment of its ethnic Chinese minority (the Hoa people) began to anger Beijing. Starting in 1977, Hanoi launched the campaign against comprador bourgeoisie. A year later, the Vietnamese Politburo announced the campaign to transform private industry and commerce. Both initiatives destroyed the Hoa people's way of life and left large swathes of their demographic impoverished. By May of 1978, 105,000 refugees including scores of Hoa people had crossed the border into China. When the land border was closed two months later, thousands took to the high seas as "boat people." As a direct response to these events, Deng Xiaoping in July 1978 canceled all aid to Vietnam.[47] These events—paired with the Vietnamese invasion of Cambodia—put Beijing in a position where action seemed to be the only recourse.

During a CCP Politburo meeting on December 31, 1979, Deng Xiaoping gave his stamp of approval for a limited punitive war against Vietnam. Alarmed by the PLA's preparation for armed conflict, the proposed invasion date was moved to mid-February.[48] This timing proved to be interesting because Deng was slated to visit the United States and meet with President Jimmy Carter. Effective January 1, 1979, the United States and PRC had formally opened diplomatic ties with one another.

As part of this move, Deng visited the United States from January 28 to February 5, 1979. During a private meeting with Carter, Deng informed Carter that he planned to "teach Vietnam a lesson."[49] Carter's national security adviser, Zbigniew Brzezinski, foresaw such an announcement from Deng. In a memo dated January 26, 1979, Brzezinski laid out talking points for Carter for when he and Deng held talks. In the memo, Brzezinski clearly enumerates the United States' aversion to military action against Vietnam: "Indicate to the Chinese ... that Chinese military action against Vietnam would jeopardize the gains we are making in isolating Vietnam in the international community."[50]

Despite this, Deng pressed Carter on the invasion. Deng expressed that it would not only be used as punishment towards Hanoi, but it would check Moscow as well: "We believe the Soviet Union will launch a war. But if we act well and properly, it is possible to postpone it. China hopes to postpone a war for twenty-two* years."[51] To President Carter and his aides that were present for this exchange, it was clear that Deng was going ahead with an invasion of Vietnam, regardless of any American objections. While Carter refused to publicly support China's proposed military action, he told Deng that he understood that Beijing could not "allow Vietnam to pursue aggression with impunity."[52] As China began its war with Vietnam two weeks later, Washington would supply Beijing with strategic intelligence regarding possible Soviet responses.[53]

---

* Rather prophetically, the Soviet Union collapsed and was dissolved in December 1991.

At 0500 hours local time on February 17, 1979, the Chinese People's Liberation Army [PLA] launched its attack into Vietnam with an opening artillery barrage focused on the village of Lang Son just over the Vietnamese border. Additional attacks were launched towards the villages of Lao Cai and Cao Bang.[54] However, the PLA forces launching the attack began to encounter serious problems. Despite brief border conflicts with India and the Soviet Union in 1962 and 1969 respectively, the PLA had not seen large conventional fighting since the Korean War of 1950–53. Additionally, the Chinese Cultural Revolution had taken a toll on the army's preparedness. During the Cultural Revolution, the Maoist objective of "political work" had taken priority over military training for conventional wars. PLA officers were co-opted as political bureaucrats rather than as military strategists.[55]

Mao's political projects during the last 10 years of his life had completely shattered the rank and command-and-control system of the PLA. In an attempt to achieve extreme levels of class abolition, Mao had virtually eliminated rank in the PLA by 1965. In the words of historian Edward C. O'Dowd, "Anything that hindered the officers from becoming close to the soldiers, or that obstructed cadres and soldiers in their efforts to become close to the masses, was to be eliminated."[56] Also, with the Soviet threat along its northern border still looming, some of the PLA's more capable fighting units, as well as the majority of its air force capabilities, were preoccupied. As such, they were not available for an armed expedition against Vietnam.[57] These disadvantages played out on the battlefields of Vietnam in February–March 1979.

Conversely, PAVN continued to follow its trend of moving away from an ideological approach to warfare to a more professional and conventional approach based on the Soviet model, which it had been doing since the late 1960s. Specialized branches, as well as a dedicated officer corps, had been slowly but surely established within PAVN over the past decade. By the time multi-front conflicts erupted in 1979, PAVN had become a competent and professional fighting force.[58]

Soviet support continued through the Chinese invasion. By the end of March 1979, the Soviets had supplied Vietnam with 400 tanks and armored personnel carriers, 400 artillery pieces, and 20 jet fighter aircraft.[59] PAVN forces during the Chinese invasion vastly outperformed much larger PLA units on the battlefield. In the area surrounding the village of Lang Son, for example, two entire Chinese field armies were held up by a single PAVN regiment. The PLA 55th Army alone, after a weeks' worth of fighting north of Lang Son, had barely managed to move 3 kilometers into Vietnam.[60] At Cao Bang, despite declaring the city previously secure, the PLA had to commit two armies to a renewed assault on the city.[61] PLA tank assaults on Cao Bang on February 20 were thrown back by withering PAVN missile barrages.[62] In Quang Ninh province during the opening hours of the invasion, a mere platoon of PAVN soldiers held up an entire Chinese regiment in its attempt to secure Cao Ba Lanh Mountain.[63]

The PLA removed its forces from Vietnam in March. By some estimates, the PLA suffered 26,000 soldiers killed, with a further 37,000 wounded in three weeks'[†] worth of fighting in the Third Indochina War (as the conflict would become known).[64] Vietnam, according to Chinese sources, suffered similar casualties.[65] Reflecting on the misguided revolutionary zeal of his country that preceded the war with Vietnam, one PLA political cadre remarked, "We were very naïve to believe our slogans would allow us to win without fighting."[66] In short, the Chinese invasion of Vietnam was a military failure.

The usage of the PLA as a political (rather than a fighting) force in the decades preceding 1979 led to a severe decline in effectiveness. In areas where the PLA outnumbered PAVN ten to one, Chinese forces still struggled to advance and hold ground. Sporadic fighting and artillery fire between Vietnam and China continued well into the 1980s, but the facts on the ground remained unchanged.[67] Crucially, the Chinese invasion did not halt, nor did it prevent the Vietnamese takeover of Cambodia. Beijing believed that by striking at Vietnam, Hanoi would either sue for a settlement in Cambodia or divert forces away from its campaign against the Khmer Rouge. However, PAVN forces in February–March 1979 kept up its offensive against the retreating forces of Pol Pot, and the Vietnamese Politburo remained unflappable.[68]

---

† To put this in perspective, roughly 58,000 Americans died in Vietnam over a 15-year period.

However, in the larger geopolitical strategic game being waged in Asia at the time, the Chinese did not come away from this conflict empty-handed. The vaunted Treaty of Friendship between Moscow and Hanoi proved to be a set of words on paper. While the Soviets launched a large military exercise (so large that the fuel reserves used for the exercise took the Soviet Ministry of Defense two years to replace) along the Chinese border in response to Beijing's aggression against Vietnam, no further action was taken.[69] For Deng, this proved that the Soviets were a "paper polar bear" and were not the threat that was previously envisioned during the dark days of fighting over Damansky Island in 1969.[70] Additionally, the Chinese invasion and subsequent skirmishing after 1979 forced Hanoi to keep a permanent force of some 700,000 troops along the northern border. Confident that the Soviet Union's unwillingness to intervene directly in 1979 highlighted a political, economic, and military decrepitude in Moscow, China began to assert itself as a major player in Asia during the 1980s.[71]

Vietnam, meanwhile, was faced with an ongoing fight in Cambodia, as well as a possible threat emanating from the north. The cost of maintaining both security efforts was too substantial for a struggling fledgling post-war economy like that of Vietnam. Accordingly, most of the cost fell on the Soviet Union, whose own economic situation in the 1980s remained unstable at best. Soviet leader Mikhail Gorbachev, who ascended to leadership in 1985, sought a rapprochement with Moscow's former enemies in Beijing. As relations between the Soviet Union and the PRC began to thaw, so too did the hardline stances of Hanoi's Politburo. After the death of Le Duan in 1986, the new leader of Vietnam Nguyen Van Linh sought to take a page out of Gorbachev's book and seek reform. Three years later in 1989, PAVN forces pulled out of Cambodia.[72] Reforms for Vietnam continued as the Cold War came to a close. Finally, thanks to its pullout from Cambodia, Hanoi was finally welcomed into the Association of Southeast Asian Nations. After the collapse of its main patron and ally, the Soviet Union, occurred in 1991, Hanoi then sought to normalize relations with Beijing. This was achieved officially in 1992.[73] Peace had finally come to Indochina.

Endnotes

Introduction

1. G. H. Turley, *The Easter Offensive: Vietnam 1972* (Novato, CA: Presidio, 1985), 134.
2. Ibid., 135.
3. V. D. Sokolovsky, ed. *Military Strategy: Soviet Doctrine and Concepts* (New York, NY: Frederick A. Praeger, 1963), 236.
4. Lien-Hang Nguyen, *Hanoi's War: An International History of the War for Peace in Vietnam* (Chapel Hill, NC: University of North Carolina Press, 2012), 7.
5. Ibid., 9.
6. Xiaobing Li, *Building Ho's Army: Chinese Military Assistance to North Vietnam* (Lexington, KY: University Press of Kentucky, 2019), 3.
7. Xiaobing Li, *The Dragon in the Jungle: The Chinese Army in the Vietnam War* (New York, NY: Oxford University Press, 2020), 226–30.
8. Qiang Zhai. *China and the Vietnam Wars, 1950–1975* (Chapel Hill, NC: University of North Carolina Press, 2000), 4–5.
9. Chen Jian, *Mao's China and the Cold War* (Chapel Hill, NC: University of North Carolina Press, 2001), 205–38.
10. An additional work regarding Soviet-Vietnamese relations vis-à-vis China: Mari Olsen, *Soviet-Vietnam Relations and the Role of China, 1949–64: Changing Alliances* (London: Routledge, 2006).
11. Ilya Gaiduk, *The Soviet Union and the Vietnam War* (Chicago: Ivan R. Dee, 1996), xv.
12. Douglas Pike, *Vietnam and the Soviet Union: Anatomy of an Alliance* (Boulder, CO: Westview Press, 1987), 79.
13. Lorenzo Lüthi, *The Sino-Soviet Split: Cold War in the Communist World* (Princeton, NJ: Princeton University Press, 2008), 330–31.
14. Dale Andradé, *Trial by Fire: The 1972 Easter Offensive, America's Last Vietnam Battle* (New York: Hippocrene Books, 1995), 536.

15 Ibid., 535–36.
16 Nguyen, 11.

Chapter 1

1   Frederik Logevall, *Embers of War: The Fall of an Empire and the Making of America's Vietnam* (New York, NY: Random House, 2012), 532–34.
2   Max Hastings, *Vietnam: An Epic Tragedy 1945–1975* (London: William Collins, 2018), 69–70.
3   Pierre Asselin, *Vietnam's American War: A History* (Cambridge, UK: Cambridge University Press, 2018), 16–19.
4   "Telegram, Mao Zedong to Liu Shaoqi," January 17, 1950, Wilson Center Digital Archive, https://digitalarchive.wilsoncenter.org/document/112657.
5   Xiaobing Li, *Building Ho's Army*, 50–53.
6   Mari Olsen, *Soviet-Vietnam Relations and the Role of China, 1949–64: Changing Alliances* (London: Routledge, 2006), 25.
7   Xiaobing Li, *Building Ho's Army*, 126–27.
8   Ibid., 144–45.
9   Ilya Gaiduk, *Confronting Vietnam: Soviet Policy toward the Indochina Conflict 1954–1963* (Washington, DC: Woodrow Wilson Center Press, 2003), 5.
10 Chen Jian, *Mao's China and the Cold War*, 120–21.
11 Douglas Pike, *Vietnam and the Soviet Union*, 33–34.
12 Christopher Goscha, "Vietnam, the Third Indochina War and the Meltdown of Asian Internationalism," in *The Third Indochina War: Conflict between China, Vietnam, and Cambodia, 1972–79*, edited by Odd Arne Westad and Sophie Quinn-Judge (London: Routledge, 2006), 158.
13 Gaiduk, *Confronting Vietnam*, 11.
14 Olsen, *Soviet-Vietnam Relations and the Role of China*, 34–35.
15 Qiang Zhai, *China and the Vietnam Wars, 1950–1975* (Chapel Hill, NC: University of North Carolina Press, 2000), 47.
16 Gaiduk, *Confronting Vietnam*, 33.
17 Pierre Asselin, *Vietnam's American War*, 72–73.
18 Logevall, *Embers of War*, 561.
19 "Telegram, Mao Zedong to Peng Dehuai and Huang Kecheng," April 28, 1954, Wilson Center Digital Archive, Mao wengao, vol. 5, 90. Translated for CWIHP by Chen Jian. https://digitalarchive.wilsoncenter.org/document/121145.
20 Ibid., 560–61.
21 Asselin, *Vietnam's American War*, 73–75.
22 Logevall, *Embers of War*, 549–50.
23 Qiang Zhai, *China and The Vietnam Wars*, 52.
24 Qiang Zhai, *China and the Vietnam Wars*, 50–51.
25 Hastings, *Vietnam*, 75.

26 Logevall, *Embers of War*, 572–73.
27 Robert Young, "HIGHT OFFICIAL HINTS OF WAR: WE MUST STOP REDS IN INDO-CHINA, HE SAYS CITES 'OBLIGATION' IF FRENCH QUIT FIGHTING." *Chicago Daily Tribune* April 17, 1954. https://www.proquest.com/historical-newspapers/hight-official-hints-war/docview/178674379/se-2.
28 John Morris, special to the *New York Times*, "NIXON IS REVEALED AS AUTHOR OF STIR OVER INDO-CHINA: VICE PRESIDENT TOLD EDITORS U.S. MIGHT INTERVENE WITH TROOPS IF THE FRENCH QUIT TRIAL BALLOON' IS SEEN STATE DEPARTMENT DECLARES IT IS 'HIGHLY UNLIKELY' FORCE WILL BE SENT TO ASIA NIXON CAUSED STIR OVER INDO-CHINA." The *New York Times*, April 18, 1954. https://www.proquest.com/historical-newspapers/nixon-is-revealed-as-author-stir-over-indo-china/docview/113095706/se-2.
29 Gaiduk, *Confronting Vietnam*, 13–19.
30 Qiang Zhai, *China and the Vietnam Wars*, 56–57.
31 Logevall, *Embers of War*, 574–76.
32 "Summary, Zhou Enlai's presentation at a meeting of the Chinese, Soviet, and Vietnamese delegations," June 15, 1954, Wilson Center Digital Archive, Zhou Enlai nianpu, 1949–1976, vol. 1, 383–84. Translated for CWIHP by Chen Jian. https://digitalarchive.wilsoncenter.org/document/121153.
33 "Telegram, Zhou Enlai to Mao Zedong, Liu Shaoqi and the CCP Central Committee, 'A Brief Report on the Meetings at Liuzhou'," July 4, 1954, Wilson Center Digital Archive, PRC FMA 206-00049-03. Translated by Chen Zhihong. https://digitalarchive.wilsoncenter.org/document/111058.
34 Hastings, *Vietnam*, 74–76.
35 "Transcript, Ho Chi Minh's presentation at the Liuzhou Conference (excerpt)," July 5, 1954, Wilson Center Digital Archive, Xiong Huayuan, Zhou Enlai chudeng shije wutai, 143–144. Translated for CWIHP by Chen Jian. https://digitalarchive.wilsoncenter.org/document/121160.
36 Gaiduk, *Confronting Vietnam*, 44–46.
37 Hastings, *Vietnam*, 77–78.
38 Logevall, *Embers of War*, 609.
39 Olsen, *Soviet-Vietnam Relations and the Role of China*, 45.
40 Chen Jian, *Mao's China and The Cold War*, 143–44.
41 "Telegram, Zhou Enlai to Mao Zedong, Liu Shaoqi, and the CCP Central Committee, Regarding the final plenary session of the conference (excerpt)," July 22, 1954, Wilson Center Digital Archive, PRC FMA 206-Y0051. Translated by Chen Jian. https://digitalarchive.wilsoncenter.org/document/121168.
42 Lien-Hang Nguyen, *Hanoi's War: An International History of the War for Peace in Vietnam* (Chapel Hill, NC: University of North Carolina Press, 2012), 30.
43 Asselin, *Vietnam's American War*, 77.
44 Qiang Zhai, *China and the Vietnam Wars*, 64.

45 Ilya Gaiduk, *The Soviet Union and the Vietnam War* (Chicago: Ivan R. Dee, 1996), 150–51.
46 Lorenzo Lüthi, *The Sino-Soviet Split*, 30–33.
47 Vladislav Zubok, *A Failed Empire: The Soviet Union in the Cold War from Stalin to Gorbachev* (Chapel Hill, NC: University of North Carolina Press, 2009), 96–98.
48 "Khrushchev's Secret Speech, 'On the Cult of Personality and Its Consequences,' Delivered at the Twentieth Party Congress of the Communist Party of the Soviet Union," February 25, 1956, Wilson Center Digital Archive, from the Congressional Record: Proceedings and Debates of the 84th Congress, 2nd Session (May 22, 1956–June 11, 1956), C11, Part 7 (June 4, 1956), 9389–403. https://digitalarchive.wilsoncenter.org/document/115995.
49 Chen Jian, *Mao's China and the Cold War*, 64–68.
50 Lüthi, *The Sino-Soviet Split*, 54–55.
51 "Working Notes from the Session of the CPSU CC Presidium on 20 October 1956," October 20, 1956, Wilson Center Digital Archive, TsKhSD, F. 3, Op. 12, D. 1005, Ll. 49–50, compiled by V. N. Malin. Published in CWIHP Bulletin 8–9, 388. https://digitalarchive.wilsoncenter.org/document/111877.
52 Lüthi, *The Sino-Soviet Split*, 54–55.
53 Ibid., 56–57.
54 Ibid., 57.
55 "Cable from the Chinese Embassy in Hungary, 'Please Inform Us of the Appropriate Attitude towards the Hungarian Events',," October 28, 1956, Wilson Center Digital Archive, PRC FMA 109–1041–01, 36. Obtained by Péter Vámos, translated by Péter Vámos and Gwenyth A. Jones. https://digitalarchive.wilsoncenter.org/document/119974.
56 Lüthi, *The Sino-Soviet Split*, 59–60; "Record of Conversation from Premier Zhou's receiving of the Hungarian Ambassador to China Ágoston Szkladán on his Farewell Visit," November 2, 1956, Wilson Center Digital Archive, PRC FMA 109–01038–02, 1–10. Translated by Péter Vámos and Gwenyth A. Jones. https://digitalarchive.wilsoncenter.org/document/117695.
57 Lüthi, *The Sino-Soviet Split*, 60–62.
58 "Record of Conversation between Polish Delegation (Gomułka et al.) and Chinese Communist Politburo Member Liu Shaoqi, Moscow," November 20, 1960, Wilson Center Digital Archive, Sygnatura XI A15, KC PZPR, AAN, Warsaw. Obtained by Douglas Selvage and translated by Malgorzata Gnoinska. https://digitalarchive.wilsoncenter.org/document/117782.
59 Lüthi, *The Sino-Soviet Split*, 112.
60 Frank Dikötter, *Mao's Great Famine: The History of China's Most Devastating Catastrophe, 1958–1962* (London: Bloomsbury Publishing, 2010), 332–33.
61 Lüthi, *The Sino-Soviet Split*, 113.

62 "Minutes of Conversation, Mao Zedong and Ambassador Yudin," July 22, 1958, Wilson Center Digital Archive, Mao Zedong waijiao wenxuan [Selected Works of Mao Zedong on Diplomacy] (Beijing: Zhongyang wenxian chubanshe, 1994), 322–33. Translated and annotated by Zhang Shu Guang and Chen Jian. https://digitalarchive.wilsoncenter.org/document/116982.
63 "Report, 'My Observations on the Soviet Union,' Zhou Enlai to Mao Zedong and the Central Leadership (Excerpt)," January 24, 1957, Wilson Center Digital Archive, Shi Zhongquan, Zhou Enlai de zhuoyue fengxian [Remarkable Achievements and Contributions of Zhou Enlai] (Beijing: Zhonggong zhongyang dangxiao chubanshe, 1993), 302–5. Translated by Zhang Shu Guang and Chen Jian. https://digitalarchive.wilsoncenter.org/document/117033.
64 Lüthi, *The Sino-Soviet Split*, 155–56.
65 Christopher Andrew, and Vasili Mitrokhin, *The World Was Going Our Way: The KGB and the Battle for the Third World* (New York, NY: Basic Books, 2005), 272–73.
66 Ibid.
67 Ibid., 253–54.
68 "Zhou Enlai's Discussion with a Kenyan African National Federation Delegation (Excerpt)," September 5, 1963, Wilson Center Digital Archive, Dang de wenxian [Party Historical Documents], no. 3 (1994): 15–16. Translated by Neil Silver. https://digitalarchive.wilsoncenter.org/document/114355.
69 Lüthi, *The Sino-Soviet Split*, 272.
70 Ibid., 272–79.
71 Sergey Radchenko, *Two Suns in the Heavens: The Sino-Soviet Struggle for Supremacy, 1962–1967* (Woodrow Wilson Center Press, 2009), 60.
72 Ibid., 61.
73 Andrew and Mitrokhin, *The World Was Going our Way*, 273.
74 Ibid., 73.
75 Nguyen, *Hanoi's War*, 34.
76 Revolts And Repressions, 2320724002. 1956, Box 07, Folder 24, Douglas Pike Collection: Unit 06—Democratic Republic of Vietnam, Vietnam Center and Sam Johnson Vietnam Archive, Texas Tech University, https://www.vietnam.ttu.edu/virtualarchive/items.php?item=2320724002.
77 Nguyen, *Hanoi's War*, 35.
78 Qiang Zhai, *China and the Vietnam Wars*, 76.
79 Ibid., 76.
80 History Of Vietnam 1954–1960: Evolution Of The War And Origins Of The Insurgency, 2321618001. 1958, Box 16, Folder 18, Douglas Pike Collection: Unit 06—Democratic Republic of Vietnam, Vietnam Center and Sam Johnson Vietnam Archive, Texas Tech University, https://www.vietnam.ttu.edu/virtualarchive/items.php?item=2321618001.

81 Hanoi's 15th Plenum resolution—May 1959 by Tai Sung An, 23130010009. January 1, 1959, Box 30, Folder 010, Douglas Pike Collection: Unit 05—National Liberation Front, Vietnam Center and Sam Johnson Vietnam Archive, Texas Tech University, https://www.vietnam.ttu.edu/virtualarchive/items.php?item=23130010009.
82 William Duiker, "Waging Revolutionary War: The Evolution of Hanoi's Strategy in the South, 1959–1965," in *The Vietnam War: Vietnamese and American Perspectives* (Armonk, NY: M. E. Sharpe, 1993), 25; J. L. S. Girling, *People's War: Conditions and Consequences in China and South East Asia* (New York, NY: Frederick A. Praeger, 1969), 12–13.
83 Duiker, "Waging Revolutionary War," 27–31.
84 Qiang Zhai, *China and the Vietnam Wars*, 89.
85 "Report from the Foreign Visitors Office of the Foreign Cultural Liaison Committee, 'The Two Major Parties of China and the Soviet Union Have Some Different Opinions, and Vietnam Faces Difficulties'," October 4, 1961, Wilson Center Digital Archive, PRC FMA 106–00661–01. Translated by Qingfei Yin. https://digitalarchive.wilsoncenter.org/document/120600.
86 Vo Ta Trong, and Tran Van Be, eds., *Lịch Sử Binh Chủng Thiết Giáp, Quân Đội Nhân Dân Việt Nam 1959–1975 [History of the Armor Branch, People's Army of Vietnam 1959–1975]*, translated by Merle Pribbenow (Hanoi: People's Army Publishing House, 1982), 9.
87 Ibid., 13–19.
88 Ibid., 21.

Chapter 2

1 Hastings, *Vietnam*, 142–53.
2 Asselin, *Vietnam's American War*, 107–8.
3 Ibid., 108–9.
4 Nguyen, *Hanoi's War*, 65.
5 Mao Tse-Tung, *On Guerilla Warfare*, translated by Samuel Griffith (Eastford, CT: Martino Fine Books, 2017), 112.
6 Nguyen, *Hanoi's War*, 66.
7 "Report, United States Military Assistance Command Vietnam—Lao Dong Central Committee Resolutions 1965–69," 1071326005. 1970, Box 13, Folder 26, Glenn Helm Collection, Vietnam Center and Sam Johnson Vietnam Archive, Texas Tech University, https://www.vietnam.ttu.edu/virtualarchive/items.php?item=1071326005.
8 Nguyen, *Hanoi's War*, 68.
9 Ibid., 68–69.
10 North Vietnam's Doctrine, 2322504003. September 23, 1964, Box 25, Folder 04, Douglas Pike Collection: Unit 06—Democratic Republic of Vietnam, Vietnam

Center and Sam Johnson Vietnam Archive, Texas Tech University, https://www.vietnam.ttu.edu/virtualarchive/items.php?item=2322504003.
11 Nguyen, *Hanoi's War*, 69–70.
12 Asselin, *Vietnam's American War*, 109–10.
13 H. R. McMaster, *Dereliction of Duty: Lyndon Johnson, Robert McNamara, the Joint Chiefs of Staff, and the Lies That Led to Vietnam* (New York, NY: Harper Perennial, 1997), 121–28.
14 Ibid., 132–33.
15 *Foreign Relations of the United States, 1964–1968*, vol. 1, Vietnam, 1964, eds. Edward Keefer and Charles Sampson (Washington, DC: Government Printing Office, 1992), Document 278.
16 Asselin, *Vietnam's American War*, 113.
17 McMaster, *Dereliction of Duty*, 125.
18 Chen Jian, *Mao's China and the Cold War*, 212.
19 "Memorandum of Conversation from the Meeting between Premier Zhou Enlai and the Algerian Ambassador to China Mohamed Yala," August 6, 1964, Wilson Center Digital Archive, PRC FMA 106–01448–02, 98–117. Translated by Jake Tompkins. https://digitalarchive.wilsoncenter.org/document/118723.
20 Chen Jian, *Mao's China and the Cold War*, 214.
21 Qiang Zhai, *China and the Vietnam Wars*, 132–33.
22 Ilya Gaiduk, *The Soviet Union and the Vietnam War*, 12–13.
23 *Foreign Relations of the United States, 1964–1968*, vol. 1, Vietnam, 1964, eds. Edward Keefer and Charles Sampson (Washington, DC: Government Printing Office, 1992), Document 295.
24 *Foreign Relations of the United States, 1964–1968*, vol. 1, Vietnam, 1964, eds. Edward Keefer and Charles Sampson (Washington, DC: Government Printing Office, 1992), Document 302.
25 Lüthi, *The Sino-Soviet Split*, 309.
26 Ibid., 309.
27 Odd Arne Westad, *The Cold War: A World History* (London: Penguin Books, 2018), 366.
28 Ibid., 367.
29 Gaiduk, *The Soviet Union and the Vietnam War*, 17.
30 "The Polyansky Report on Khrushchev's Mistakes in Foreign Policy, October 1964," October 1964, Wilson Center Digital Archive, Library of Congress, Manuscript Division, Dmitriĭ Antonovich Volkogonov papers, 1887–1995, mm97083838, Reel 18. Translated by Svetlana Savranskaya, The National Security Archive. https://digitalarchive.wilsoncenter.org/document/115108.
31 Zubok, *A Failed Empire*, 197.
32 Lüthi, *The Sino-Soviet Split*, 311.
33 Zubok, *A Failed Empire*, 197–98.
34 Lüthi, *The Sino-Soviet Split*, 289.

35 Ibid., 290.
36 Radchenko, *Two Suns in the Heavens*, 134.
37 Ibid., 134.
38 Lüthi, *The Sino-Soviet Split*, 292.
39 "Note No. 2/65 on Conversations with Comrade Shcherbakov about the Developmental Tendencies in the Democratic Republic of Vietnam, on 22 and 28 December 1964," January 6, 1965, Wilson Center Digital Archive, SAPMO-BArch, DY 30/IV A 2/20/442, 8–10. Translated from German by Lorenz Lüthi. https://digitalarchive.wilsoncenter.org/document/117710.
40 Radchenko, *Two Suns in the Heavens*, 109–10.
41 Asselin, *Vietnam's American War*, 118–19.
42 "Zhou Enlai Talking to Ho Chi Minh," March 1, 1965, Wilson Center Digital Archive, CWIHP Working Paper 22, "77 Conversations." https://digitalarchive.wilsoncenter.org/document/113055.
43 "Cable from the Chinese Embassy in the Soviet Union, 'Recent Responses from the Soviet Revisionists to the Situation in Vietnam'," April 10, 1965, Wilson Center Digital Archive, PRC FMA 109–03654–02, 9–12. Translated by David Cowhig. https://digitalarchive.wilsoncenter.org/document/118725.
44 Nicholas Khoo, *Collateral Damage: Sino-Soviet Rivalry and the Termination of Tthe Sino-Vietnamese Alliance* (New York, NY: Columbia University Press, 2011), 25–27.
45 Pike, *Vietnam and the Soviet Union*, 121.
46 "Discussion between Zhou Enlai and Pham Van Dong," October 9, 1965, Wilson Center Digital Archive, CWIHP Working Paper 22, "77 Conversations." https://digitalarchive.wilsoncenter.org/document/113065.
47 Frank Dikötter, *The Cultural Revolution: A People's History, 1962–1976* (New York, NY: Bloomsbury Publishing, 2019), xiii.
48 Ibid., xii.
49 Ibid., 11.
50 Robert Service, *Comrades: A History of World Communism.* (Cambridge, MA: Harvard University Press, 2010), 335.
51 Radchenko, *Two Suns in the Heavens*, 176.
52 Ibid., xv.
53 Service, *Comrades*, 336–38.
54 Radchenko, *Two Suns in the Heavens*, 178–80.
55 Dikötter, *The Cultural Revolution*, xv.
56 Dikötter, *The Cultural Revolution*, 174–75.
57 Ibid., 177–80.
58 "Discussion between Zhou Enlai and Le Duan," March 23, 1966, Wilson Center Digital Archive, CWIHP Working Paper 22, "77 Conversations." https://digitalarchive.wilsoncenter.org/document/113069.
59 Radchenko, *Two Suns in the Heavens*, 172.
60 Westad, *The Cold War*, 333.
61 Khoo, *Collateral Damage*, 35–36.

62 Qiang Zhai, *China and the Vietnam Wars*, 150–51.
63 Pike, *Vietnam and the Soviet Union*, 123.
64 Dikötter, *The Cultural Revolution*, 157.
65 Xiaobing Li, *The Dragon in the Jungle: The Chinese Army in the Vietnam War* (New York, NY: Oxford University Press, 2020), 149.
66 Asselin, *Vietnam's American War*, 149–53.
67 Qiang Zhai, *China and the Vietnam Wars*, 177.
68 Khoo, *Collateral Damage*, 36–38.
69 Asselin, *Vietnam's American War*, 155–56.
70 John Cash, John Albright, and Allan Sandstrum, *Seven Firefights in Vietnam* (Mineola, NY: Dover Publications, 2007), 129–31.
71 William Phillips, *Night of the Silver Stars: The Battle of Lang Vei* (Annapolis, MD: Naval Institute Press, 1997), 2–3.
72 Ibid., 14.
73 Ibid., 22–23.
74 Ibid., 58–69.
75 Ibid., 70.
76 Cash et al., *Seven Firefights in Vietnam*, 127–28.
77 David Rosser-Owen, *Vietnam Weapons Handbook* (Wellingborough, UK: Patrick Stephens Limited, 1986), 112–13.
78 Phillips, *Night of the Silver Stars*, 76–77.
79 Joseph Galloway, Interview with Dennis Thompson, Army, October 17, 2018. The United States of American Vietnam War Commemoration. https://www.vietnamwar50th.com/history_and_legacy/oral_history/thompson,-dennis/.
80 Phillips, *Night of the Silver Stars*, 85.
81 Cash et al., *Seven Firefights in Vietnam*, 149–53.
82 Cash et al., *Seven Firefights in Vietnam*, 162–63.
83 Asselin, *Vietnam's American War*, 158.
84 "Combat After Action Report—Battle of Lang Vei, 5th Special Forces Group (Airborne). 1st Special Forces, Period January 24–February 7, 1968 (U)—U.S. Army," 1071806001. August 12, 1968, Box 18, Folder 06, Glenn Helm Collection, Vietnam Center and Sam Johnson Vietnam Archive, Texas Tech University, https://www.vietnam.ttu.edu/virtualarchive/items.php?item=1071806001.
85 Phillips, *Night of the Silver Stars*, 130–31.
86 Simon Dunstan, *Vietnam Tracks: Armor in Battle 1945–1975* (Novato, CA: Presidio Press, 1982), 183.
87 Asselin, *Vietnam's American War*, 158.
88 Gregory Daddis, *Withdrawal: Reassessing America's Final Years in Vietnam* (New York, NY: Oxford University Press, 2017), 35–50.
89 James Willbanks, *A Raid Too Far: Operation Lam Son 719 and Vietnamization in Laos* (College Station, TX: Texas A&M University Press, 2014), 8–9.
90 Ibid., 12–14.
91 Ibid., 20–21.

92 Ibid., 22–23
93 Ibid., 34–35.
94 Ibid., 62–65.
95 Vo Ta Trong, and Tran Van Be, eds., *Lịch Sử Binh Chủng Thiết Giáp, Quân Đội Nhân Dân Việt Nam 1959–1975* [*History of the Armor Branch, People's Army of Vietnam 1959–1975*], translated by Merle Pribbenow (Hanoi: People's Army Publishing House, 1982), 85.
96 Donn Starry, *Mounted Combat in Vietnam* (Washington, DC: Department of the Army, 1978), 191.
97 Ibid., 193.
98 Assessment of Ho Chi Minh Trail Operation: March–April 1971, 2122004034. April 10, 1971, Box 20, Folder 04, Douglas Pike Collection: Unit 01—Assessment and Strategy, Vietnam Center and Sam Johnson Vietnam Archive, Texas Tech University, https://www.vietnam.ttu.edu/virtualarchive/items.php?item=2122004034.
99 Willbanks, *A Raid Too Far*, 128–30.
100 Starry, *Mounted Combat in Vietnam*, 195–96.
101 Ibid., 194.
102 "CHECO Reports #135; Lam Son 719 The South Vietnamese Incursion into Laos; January 30–March 24, 1971; March 24, 1971," 0390109001. March 24, 1971, Box 01, Folder 09, Contemporary Historical Examination of Current Operations (CHECO) Reports of Southeast Asia (1961–75), Vietnam Center and Sam Johnson Vietnam Archive, Texas Tech University, https://www.vietnam.ttu.edu/virtualarchive/items.php?item=0390109001.
103 Willbanks, *A Raid Too Far*, 175.
104 *Quan Doi Nhan Dan* on PLAF Successes in 1971, 2122010053. July 30, 1971, Box 20, Folder 10, Douglas Pike Collection: Unit 01—Assessment and Strategy, Vietnam Center and Sam Johnson Vietnam Archive, Texas Tech University, https://www.vietnam.ttu.edu/virtualarchive/items.php?item=2122010053.

Chapter 3

1 Working Paper—The Power Struggle in North Vietnam, 24991810007. Vietnam Center and Sam Johnson Vietnam Archive. Undated, Box 18, Folder 10, Dale W. Andrade Collection, Vietnam Center and Sam Johnson Vietnam Archive, Texas Tech University, https://www.vietnam.ttu.edu/virtualarchive/items.php?item=24991810007.
2 Andradé, *Trial by Fire*, 39–40.
3 Chen Jian, *Mao's China and the Cold War*, 234
4 "Mao Zedong's Talk at a Meeting of the Central Cultural Revolution Group (Excerpt)," March 15, 1969, Wilson Center Digital Archive, Zhonghua renmin gongheguo shilu [A Factual History of the People's Republic of China] (Changchun: Jilin renmin chubanshe, 1994), vol. 3, part 1, 467–69. https://digitalarchive.wilsoncenter.org/document/111241.

5   "Minutes of Conversation between Ion Gheorghe Maurer, Paul Niculescu Mizil, Zhou Enlai, and Li Xiannian on 7 September 1969," September 7, 1969, Wilson Center Digital Archive, A.N.I.C., fond CC of RCP—External Relations Division, file 72/1969, 4–30, in Relatiile Romano-Chineze, 1880–1974 [Sino-Romanian Relations, 1880–1974], edited by Ioan Romulus Budura (Bucharest, 2005), 943–59. Translated by Madalina Cristoloveanu. https://digitalarchive.wilsoncenter.org/document/117758.
6   Chen Jian, *Mao's China and the Cold War*, 240–45.
7   "Report by Four Chinese Marshals, Chen Yi, Ye Jianying, Nie Rongzhen, and Xu Xiangqian, to the Central Committee, 'Our Views about the Current Situation' (Excerpt)," September 17, 1969, Wilson Center Digital Archive, Zhonggong dangshi ziliao, no. 42 (June 1992), 84–86. Translated for CWIHP by Chen Jian with assistance from Li Di. https://digitalarchive.wilsoncenter.org/document/117154.
8   *Foreign Relations of the United States, 1969–1976*, vol. 17, China, 1969–1972, eds. Stephen E. Phillips and Edward C. Keefer (Washington, DC: Government Printing Office, 2010), Document 105.
9   *Foreign Relations of the United States, 1969–1976*, vol. 17, China, 1969–1972, eds. Stephen E. Phillips and Edward C. Keefer (Washington, DC: Government Printing Office, 2010), Document 104.
10 Qiang Zhai, *China and the Vietnam Wars*, 194–95.
11 "Discussion between Zhou Enlai, Le Duan, and Pham Van Dong," March 7, 1971, Wilson Center Digital Archive, CWIHP Working Paper 22, "77 Conversations." https://digitalarchive.wilsoncenter.org/document/113108.
12 Qiang Zhai, *China and the Vietnam Wars*, 195–96.
13 *Foreign Relations of the United States, 1969–1976*, vol. 17, China, 1969–1972, eds. Stephen E. Phillips and Edward C. Keefer (Washington, DC: Government Printing Office, 2010), Document 139.
14 Qiang Zhai, *China and the Vietnam Wars*, 200.
15 Andrew and Mitrokhin, *The World Was Going our Way*, 281.
16 "Joint Communique between the United States and China," February 27, 1972, Wilson Center Digital Archive, Nixon Presidential Library and Museum, Staff Member Office Files (SMOF), President's Personal Files (PPF), Box 73. https://digitalarchive.wilsoncenter.org/document/121325.
17 Qiang Zhai, *China and the Vietnam Wars*, 200.
18 *Foreign Relations of the United States, 1969–1976*, vol. 12, Soviet Union, January 1969–October 1970, eds. Erin Mahan and Edward Keefer (Washington, DC: Government Printing Office, 2010), Document 14.
19 Zubok, *A Failed Empire*, 216.
20 *Foreign Relations of the United States, 1969–1976*, vol. 13, Soviet Union, October 1970–October 1971, eds. David Geyer and Edward C. Keefer (Washington, DC: Government Printing Office, 2011), Document 309.
21 David Kraslow, "Nixon Will Visit Moscow in May: Summit Talks to Review 'all Major Issues' MOSCOW TALKS." The *Los Angeles Times*, October 13,1971, 3-a1.

https://www.proquest.com/historical-newspapers/nixon-will-visit-moscow-may/docview/156806221/se-2.

22 "Discussion between Zhou Enlai and Le Duan," July 13, 1971, Wilson Center Digital Archive, CWIHP Working Paper 22, "77 Conversations." https://digitalarchive.wilsoncenter.org/document/113109.

23 "Discussion between Chen Yi and Le Duc Tho," October 17, 1968, Wilson Center Digital Archive, CWIHP Working Paper 22, "77 Conversations." https://digitalarchive.wilsoncenter.org/document/112180.

24 Asselin, *Vietnam's American War*, 186–92.

25 Grasp the Strategic Opportunity, 2122304036. Vietnam Center and Sam Johnson Vietnam Archive. April 1972, Box 23, Folder 04, Douglas Pike Collection: Unit 01—Assessment and Strategy, Vietnam Center and Sam Johnson Vietnam Archive, Texas Tech University, https://www.vietnam.ttu.edu/virtualarchive/items.php?item=2122304036.

26 Operational Analyses, Rand Corporation—Giap and the Seventh Son—re: Analysis of General Giap's Spring Offensive, 24991810003. Vietnam Center and Sam Johnson Vietnam Archive. Undated, Box 18, Folder 10, Dale W. Andrade Collection, Vietnam Center and Sam Johnson Vietnam Archive, Texas Tech University, https://www.vietnam.ttu.edu/virtualarchive/items.php?item=24991810003.

27 "COMMUNIST MILITARY AND ECONOMIC AID TO NORTH VIETNAM, 1970–1974," Central Intelligence Agency, 1975. Freedom of Information Act Electronic Reading Room. https://www.cia.gov/readingroom/document/0001166499.

28 Andradé, *Trial by Fire*, 40–41.

29 Conflict studies: North Vietnam's blitzkrieg, 2131903007. Vietnam Center and Sam Johnson Vietnam Archive. Undated, Box 19, Folder 03, Douglas Pike Collection: Unit 02—Military Operations, Vietnam Center and Sam Johnson Vietnam Archive, Texas Tech University, https://www.vietnam.ttu.edu/virtualarchive/items.php?item=2131903007.

30 Study Of Military Information On The 5th Battalion, 203rd Armored Regiment, PAVN Armor Command, On The An Loc Battlefield, 2321317001. Vietnam Center and Sam Johnson Vietnam Archive. 13 April 1972, Box 13, Folder 17, Douglas Pike Collection: Unit 06 - Democratic Republic of Vietnam, Vietnam Center and Sam Johnson Vietnam Archive, Texas Tech University, https://www.vietnam.ttu.edu/virtualarchive/items.php?item=2321317001.

31 Information On The 2nd T54 Tank Company, 1st Battalion, 203rd PAVN Armored Regiment, Participating In Combat On The Kontum City Front, 2321317004. Vietnam Center and Sam Johnson Vietnam Archive. May 18, 1972, Box 13, Folder 17, Douglas Pike Collection: Unit 06—Democratic Republic of Vietnam, Vietnam Center and Sam Johnson Vietnam Archive, Texas Tech University, https://www.vietnam.ttu.edu/virtualarchive/items.php?item=2321317004.

32 Infiltration Routes Used By PAVN Tanks To Penetrate The Quang Tri Battlefield And Organization And Activities Of The 203rd PAVN Armored Regiment,

2321317003. Vietnam Center and Sam Johnson Vietnam Archive. April 9, 1972, Box 13, Folder 17, Douglas Pike Collection: Unit 06—Democratic Republic of Vietnam, Vietnam Center and Sam Johnson Vietnam Archive, Texas Tech University, https://www.vietnam.ttu.edu/virtualarchive/items.php?item=2321317003.

33 Stephen Randolph, *Powerful and Brutal Weapons: Nixon, Kissinger, and the Easter Offensive* (Cambridge, MA: Harvard University Press, 2007), 35–36.

34 Stephen Randolph, "A Bigger Game: Nixon, Kissinger, and the 1972 Easter Offensive" (George Washington University, 2005), 60.

35 Infiltration Routes Used By PAVN Tanks To Penetrate The Quang Tri Battlefield And Organization And Activities Of The 203rd PAVN Armored Regiment, 2321317003. Vietnam Center and Sam Johnson Vietnam Archive. 09 April 1972, Box 13, Folder 17, Douglas Pike Collection: Unit 06—Democratic Republic of Vietnam, Vietnam Center and Sam Johnson Vietnam Archive, Texas Tech University, https://www.vietnam.ttu.edu/virtualarchive/items.php?item=2321317003.

36 Information On The Activities Of The 2nd And 12th Companies, 1st Battalion, 203rd Armored Regiment, In B3 Front, 2321317006. Vietnam Center and Sam Johnson Vietnam Archive. June 3, 1972, Box 13, Folder 17, Douglas Pike Collection: Unit 06Democratic Republic of Vietnam, Vietnam Center and Sam Johnson Vietnam Archive, Texas Tech University, https://www.vietnam.ttu.edu/virtualarchive/items.php?item=2321317006.

37 "Report, MACV J2—The Tank Battles at Dong Ha—re: 20th ARVN Tank Regiment battles," 24991908009. Vietnam Center and Sam Johnson Vietnam Archive. Undated, Box 19, Folder 08, Dale W. Andrade Collection, Vietnam Center and Sam Johnson Vietnam Archive, Texas Tech University, https://www.vietnam.ttu.edu/virtualarchive/items.php?item=24991908009.

38 Andradé, *Trial by Fire*, 536.

39 Stephen Emerson, *North Vietnam's 1972 Easter Offensive: Hanoi's Gamble* (Yorkshire, UK: Pen and Sword Books, 2020), 31–32.

40 Tran Van Nhut, and Christian Arevian, *An Loc: The Unfinished War* (Lubbock, TX: Texas Tech University Press, 2009), 117–19.

41 Determined to Completely Defeat the Enemy During the Nguyen Hue Campaign, 2122302014. Vietnam Center and Sam Johnson Vietnam Archive. April 1, 1972, Box 23, Folder 02, Douglas Pike Collection: Unit 01—Assessment and Strategy, Vietnam Center and Sam Johnson Vietnam Archive, Texas Tech University, https://www.vietnam.ttu.edu/virtualarchive/items.php?item=2122302014.

42 Turley, *The Easter Offensive*, 126–34.

43 Memo from Senior Advisor 3rd VNMC Marine Infantry Battalion to Senior Marine Advisor—re: Evaluation of the PAVN Easter '72 Offensive, 24991909035. Undated, Box 19, Folder 09, Dale W. Andrade Collection, Vietnam Center and Sam Johnson Vietnam Archive, Texas Tech University, https://www.vietnam.ttu.edu/virtualarchive/items.php?item=24991909035.

44 Turley, *The Easter Offensive*, 135.

45 James Willbanks, *Abandoning Vietnam: How America Left and South Vietnam Lost Its War* (Lawrence, KS: University Press of Kansas, 2004), 133–35.
46 James Willbanks, *The Battle of An Loc* (Bloomington, IN: Indiana University Press, 2005), 152–61.
47 Max Hastings, *Vietnam: An Epic Tragedy 1945–1975* (William Collins, 2018), 540.
48 Ibid., 541.
49 Ibid., 540.
50 Ngo Quang Truong, *The Easter Offensive of 1972* (Washington, DC: U.S. Army Center of Military History, 1980), 112.
51 Ibid., 31.
52 Ibid., 29–31
53 Ibid., 160.
54 Ibid., 159–60.
55 Thomas McKenna, *Kontum: The Battle to Save South Vietnam* (Lexington, KY: University Press of Kentucky, 2011), 170–73.
56 Message from John Vann to Creighton Abrams—re: Daily Commander's Evaluation, May 26, 1972, 24992403013. Undated, Box 24, Folder 3, Dale W. Andrade Collection, Vietnam Center and Sam Johnson Vietnam Archive, Texas Tech University, https://www.vietnam.ttu.edu/virtualarchive/items.php?item=24992403013.
57 Willbanks, *The Battle of An Loc*, 153.
58 "Translated Report—re: On the Final Analysis of Offensive Operations in South Vietnam and Requirements for the future Armed Struggle," 11271625003. Vietnam Center and Sam Johnson Vietnam Archive. July 2, 1993, Box 16, Folder 25, Garnett Bell Collection, Vietnam Center and Sam Johnson Vietnam Archive, Texas Tech University, https://www.vietnam.ttu.edu/virtualarchive/items.php?item=11271625003.
59 Merle Pribbenow, trans., *Victory in Vietnam: The Official History of the People's Army of Vietnam, 1954–1975* (Lawrence, KS: University Press of Kansas., 2002), 297–98.
60 PAVN Memorandum on Failure to Capture An Loc: May—re: Nguyen Hue Campaign, 2122401007. Vietnam Center and Sam Johnson Vietnam Archive. May 1972, Box 24, Folder 01, Douglas Pike Collection: Unit 01—Assessment and Strategy, Vietnam Center and Sam Johnson Vietnam Archive, Texas Tech University, https://www.vietnam.ttu.edu/virtualarchive/items.php?item=2122401007.
61 "Report, Briefing Material—re: Review of PAVN Armor Tactics and Training—Record of MACV Part 2," F015900190228. Vietnam Center and Sam Johnson Vietnam Archive. November 8, 1972, Box 0019, Folder 0228, Sam Johnson Vietnam Archive Collection, Vietnam Center and Sam Johnson Vietnam Archive, Texas Tech University, https://www.vietnam.ttu.edu/virtualarchive/items.php?item=F015900190228.
62 "Report, Intelligence Directorate—The Nguyen-Hue Offensive—Record of MACV Part 1," F015800210009. Vietnam Center and Sam Johnson Vietnam Archive. January 12, 1973, Box 0021, Folder 0009, Sam Johnson Vietnam Archive Collection,

Vietnam Center and Sam Johnson Vietnam Archive, Texas Tech University, https://www.vietnam.ttu.edu/virtualarchive/items.php?item=F015800210009.
63 Ibid.

Chapter 4

1 This section borrows heavily from a conference paper written by the author for the Institute for Peace and Conflict Conference in Lubbock, Texas, in March 2023: James Pomeroy, "Victims of Peace: Comparing and Contrasting the Paris Peace Accords (1973) and the Doha Agreement (2020)," in *Comparison and Discourse: The Comparative Legacy America's War in Vietnam* (Lubbock, TX: Texas Tech University's Institute for Peace and Conflict, 2023).
2 Asselin, *Vietnam's American War*, 168.
3 Gaiduk, *The Soviet Union and the Vietnam War*, 156–58.
4 Asselin, *Vietnam's American War*, 170–71.
5 Larry Berman, *No Peace, No Honor: Nixon, Kissinger, & Betrayal in Vietnam* (New York: The Free Press, 2001), 32–36.
6 Daddis, *Withdrawal*, 50.
7 Ken Hughes, *Fatal Politics: The Nixon Tapes, The Vietnam War, and the Casualties of Reelection* (Charlottesville, VA: University of Virginia Press, 2015), 28–31.
8 Ibid., 189–92.
9 David Goldman, and Erin Mahan, eds., *Foreign Relations of the United States, 1969–1976*, vol. 7, Vietnam, July 1970–72, (Washington, DC: Government Printing Office, 2010), Document 170.
10 Hastings, *Vietnam: An Epic Tragedy*, 517.
11 Arnold Isaacs, *Without Honor: Defeat in Vietnam and Cambodia* (Baltimore, MD: The Johns Hopkins University Press, 1983), 28–29.
12 Ibid., 39.
13 John Carland, and Edward Keefer, eds., *Foreign Relations of the United States, 1969–1976*, vol. 9, Vietnam, October 1972–January 1973 (Washington, DC: Government Printing Office, 2010), Document 168.
14 Isaacs, *Without Honor*, 52–57.
15 John Carland, and Edward Keefer, eds., *Foreign Relations of the United States, 1969–1976*, vol. 9, Vietnam, October 1972–January 1973 (Washington, DC: Government Printing Office, 2010), Document 206.
16 Hughes, *Fatal Politics*, 193.
17 George Veith, *Black April: The Fall of South Vietnam 1973–75* (New York, NY: Encounter Books, 2012), 19–21.
18 PRGRSV Spokesman Accuses U.S., RVN of Cease-Fire Violations—Paris AFP, 2132210046. 12 February 1973, Box 22, Folder 10, Douglas Pike Collection: Unit 02—Military Operations, Vietnam Center and Sam Johnson Vietnam Archive, Texas Tech University, https://www.vietnam.ttu.edu/virtualarchive/items.php?item=2132210046.

19 Van Tien Dung, *Our Great Spring Victory: An Account of the Liberation of South Vietnam* (New York: Monthly Review Press, 1977), 7.
20 Veith, *Black April*, 45–46.
21 "Resolution of the 21st Plenum of the Party Central Committee, No. 227-NQ/TW (Excerpts)," October 13, 1973, Wilson Center Digital Archive, Dang Cong san Viet Nam, Van Kien Dang Toan tap [Party Documents Complete Series], vol. 34 (Hanoi: Nha xuat ban Chinh tri quoc gia, 2004), 210–61. Translated by Merle Pribbenow. https://digitalarchive.wilsoncenter.org/document/175857.
22 Veith, *Black April*, 46.
23 Hastings, *Vietnam: An Epic Tragedy*, 590.
24 Dung, *Our Great Spring Victory*, 19.
25 Hastings, *Vietnam: An Epic Tragedy*, 590.
26 "COMMUNIST MILITARY AND ECONOMIC AID TO NORTH VIETNAM, 1970–1974," Central Intelligence Agency, 1975. Freedom of Information Act Electronic Reading Room. https://www.cia.gov/readingroom/document/0001166499.
27 Asselin, *Vietnam's American War*, 219–20.
28 Dung, *Our Great Spring Victory*, 11.
29 Asselin, *Vietnam's American War*, 223–24.
30 Hastings, *Vietnam: An Epic Tragedy*, 592–93.
31 "Politburo Resolution No. 236-NQ/TW," August 13, 1974, Wilson Center Digital Archive, Dang Cong san Viet Nam, Van Kien Dang Toan tap [Party Documents Complete Series], vol. 35 (Hanoi: Nha xuat ban Chinh tri quoc gia, 2004), 116–23. Translated by Merle Pribbenow. https://digitalarchive.wilsoncenter.org/document/175861.
32 "NIE 53/14.3–1-74 THE LIKELIHOOD OF A MAJOR NORTH VIETNAMESE OFFENSIVE AGAINST SOUTH VIETNAM," Central Intelligence Agency, May 23, 1974. Freedom of Information Act Electronic Reading Room. https://www.cia.gov/readingroom/document/0001166463.
33 Hastings, *Vietnam: An Epic Tragedy*, 593.
34 Veith, *Black April*, 103–8.
35 Ibid., 111–12.
36 Dung, *Our Great Spring Victory*, 23.
37 Ibid., 26–28.
38 Hastings, *Vietnam: An Epic Tragedy*, 597.
39 Dung, *Our Great Spring Victory*, 45.
40 Hastings, *Vietnam: An Epic Tragedy*, 598–99.
41 Ha Mai Viet, *Steel and Blood: South Vietnamese Armor and the War for Southeast Asia* (Annapolis, MD: Naval Institute Press, 2008), 201–2.
42 Ibid., 204.
43 Memo from Moncrieff J. Spear, Consul General, Nha Trang to Ambassador Graham Martin—The Communist Offensive in Region Two—Part 1 of 2, 10840101003.

[Ca. April 1975], Box 01, Folder 01, Moncrieff J. Spear Collection, Vietnam Center and Sam Johnson Vietnam Archive, Texas Tech University, https://www.vietnam.ttu.edu/virtualarchive/items.php?item=10840101003.
44 "Cable No. 38B from Brother Chien [Vo Nguyen Giap] to Brother Tuan [Van Tien Dung]," March 22, 1975, Wilson Center Digital Archive, Dai Thang Mua Xuan, 1975: Van Kien Dang [Great Spring Victory, 1975: Party Documents] (Hanoi: Nha xuat ban Chinh tri quoc gia, 2005), 166–67. Translated by Merle Pribbenow. https://digitalarchive.wilsoncenter.org/document/175988.
45 Dung, *Our Great Spring Victory*, 102–9.
46 Hastings, *Vietnam: An Epic Tragedy*, 607.
47 Ibid., 610–11.
48 Veith, *Black April*, 420–31.
49 Viet, *Steel and Blood*, 238.
50 "Cable No. 10/TT.75, KBN [COSVN] Party Current Affairs Committee Circular," April 22, 1975, Wilson Center Digital Archive, Dai Thang Mua Xuan, 1975: Van Kien Dang [Great Spring Victory, 1975: Party Documents] (Hanoi: Nha xuat ban Chinh tri quoc gia, 2005), 302–4. Translated by Merle Pribbenow. https://digitalarchive.wilsoncenter.org/document/176150.
51 Viet, *Steel and Blood*, 240.
52 Ibid., 240–53.
53 Ibid., 258.
54 David Henley, "Tank 843 Made History in Saigon 40 Years Ago," *The Nevada Appeal*, April 23, 2015. https://www.nevadaappeal.com/news/2015/apr/23/tank-843-made-history-in-saigon-40-years-ago/.

Epilogue

1 Edward O'Dowd, *Chinese Military Strategy in the Third Indochina War: The Last Maoist War* (London: Routledge, 2007), 35.
2 Qiang Zhai, *China and the Vietnam Wars*, 213.
3 "Discussion between Mao Zedong and Le Duan," September 24, 1975, Wilson Center Digital Archive, CWIHP Working Paper 22, "77 Conversations." https://digitalarchive.wilsoncenter.org/document/111263.
4 Robert Service, *Comrades: A History of World Communism* (Cambridge, MA: Harvard University Press, 2007), 339; Dikötter, *The Cultural Revolution*, 304–5.
5 Dikötter, *The Cultural Revolution*, 303–7.
6 Ibid., 307–13.
7 Ibid., 315–16.
8 Service, *Comrades*, 438.
9 Zhang Xiaoming, "Deng Xiaoping and China's Decision to Go to War with Vietnam," *Journal of Cold War Studies* 12, no. 3 (Summer 2010), 9–10.

10 Stephen Morris, *Why Vietnam Invaded Cambodia: Political Culture and the Causes of War* (Stanford, CA: Stanford University Press, 1999), 213–14.
11 Ibid., 215.
12 Asselin, *Vietnam's American War*, 239–40.
13 Qiang Zhai, *China and the Vietnam Wars*, 214.
14 O'Dowd, *Chinese Military Strategy in the Third Indochina War*, 40–41.
15 Morris, *Why Vietnam Invaded Cambodia*, 70–71.
16 Ben Kiernan, *Blood and Soil: A World History of Genocide and Extermination from Sparta to Darfur* (New Haven, CT: Yale University Press, 2007), 547.
17 Service, *Comrades*, 405.
18 Ben Kiernan, *The Pol Pot Regime: Race, Power, and Genocide in Cambodia under the Khmer Rouge, 1975–79* (Third. New Haven, CT: Yale University Press, 2008), 62–64.
19 Morris, *Why Vietnam Invaded Cambodia*, 23–25.
20 Ibid., 43–46.
21 Morris, *Why Vietnam Invaded Cambodia*, 47–49; Sergey Radchenko, *Unwanted Visionaries: The Soviet Failure in Asia at the End of the Cold War* (New York, NY: Oxford University Press, 2014), 125–26.
22 Morris, *Why Vietnam Invaded Cambodia*, 54–60.
23 Ibid., 31–65.
24 Kiernan, *Blood and Soil*, 549.
25 Kiernan, *The Pol Pot Regime*, 264–93.
26 Ibid., 295.
27 Ibid., 195–203.
28 Service, *Comrades*, 406.
29 Kiernan, *The Pol Pot Regime*, 460.
30 Ibid., 373–79.
31 Kiernan, *Blood and Soil*, 553.
32 Edward O'Dowd, *Chinese Military Strategy in the Third Indochina War: The Last Maoist War* (London: Routledge, 2007), 37.
33 Morris, *Why Vietnam Invaded Cambodia*, 107.
34 Kiernan, *Blood and Soil*, 553.
35 Ibid., 552.
36 Morris, *Why Vietnam Invaded Cambodia*, 185.
37 Ibid., 186.
38 Ibid., 185–86.
39 Ibid., 212.
40 Ibid., 108.
41 O'Dowd, *Chinese Military Strategy in the Third Indochina War*, 37–38.
42 Ibid., 38–39.
43 Sophie Quinn-Judge, "Victory on the Battlefield; Isolation in Asia: Vietnam's Cambodia Decade, 1979–1989," in *The Third Indochina War: Conflict between*

China, Vietnam, and Cambodia, 1972–79, edited by Odd Arne Westad and Sophie Quinn-Judge (London: Routledge, 2006), 213.
44 O'Dowd, *Chinese Military Strategy in the Third Indochina War*, 39.
45 Asselin, *Vietnam's American War*, 241–42.
46 O'Dowd, *Chinese Military Strategy in the Third Indochina War*, 41–42.
47 Ibid., 42–43.
48 Xiaoming, "Deng Xiaoping and China's Decision to go to War with Vietnam," 19–22.
49 John Cooper, "The Sino-Vietnam War's Thirtieth Anniversary," *American Journal of Chinese Studies* 16, no. 1 (April 2009) 73.
50 *Foreign Relations of the United States, 1977–1980*, vol. 22, Southeast Asia and the Pacific, David P. Nickles and Melissa Jane Taylor, eds., (Washington, DC: Government Printing Office, 2017), Document 41.
51 Westad, *The Cold War*, 491.
52 Ibid., 491.
53 Cooper, "The Sino-Vietnam War's Thirtieth Anniversary," 73.
54 O'Dowd, *Chinese Military Strategy in the Third Indochina War*, 58–79.
55 Ibid., 27–28.
56 Ibid., 126.
57 Bruce Elleman, *Modern Chinese Warfare. 1795–1989* (London: Routledge, 2001), 292.
58 O'Dowd, *Chinese Military Strategy in the Third Indochina War*, 151.
59 Radchenko, *Unwanted Visionaries*, 128.
60 O'Dowd, *Chinese Military Strategy in the Third Indochina War*, 46–57.
61 Ibid., 46.
62 Ibid., 60.
63 Ibid., 46.
64 Elleman, *Modern Chinese Warfare*, 293.
65 Asselin, *Vietnam's American War*, 242–43; Elleman, *Modern Chinese Warfare*, 293.
66 O'Dowd, *Chinese Military Strategy in the Third Indochina War*, 142.
67 Ibid., 154–55.
68 Ibid., 72.
69 Radchenko, *Unwanted Visionaries*, 128.
70 Cooper, *The Sino-Vietnam War's Thirtieth Anniversary*, 73.
71 Elleman, *Modern Chinese Warfare*, 295.
72 Radchenko, *Unwanted Visionaries*, 131–58.
73 Westad, *The Cold War*, 563.

Bibliography

All hyperlinks cited in this bibliography accessed between January 1, 2022 and October 31, 2024.

Primary Sources (Published)

Dung, Van Tien. *Our Great Spring Victory: An Account of the Liberation of South Vietnam.* New York: Monthly Review Press, 1977.

Henley, David. "Tank 843 Made History in Saigon 40 Years Ago." *Nevada Appeal*, April 23, 2015. https://www.nevadaappeal.com/news/2015/apr/23/tank-843-made-history-in-saigon-40-years-ago/.

Pribbenow, Merle, trans. *Victory in Vietnam: The Official History of the People's Army of Vietnam, 1954–1975.* Lawrence, KS: University Press of Kansas, 2002.

Sokolovsky, V. D., ed. *Military Strategy: Soviet Doctrine and Concepts.* New York, NY: Frederick A. Praeger, 1963.

Trong, Vo Ta, and Tran Van Be, eds. *Lịch Sử Binh Chủng Thiết Giáp, Quân Đội Nhân Dân Việt Nam 1959–1975* [*History of the Armor Branch, People's Army of Vietnam 1959–1975*]. Translated by Merle Pribbenow. Hanoi: People's Army Publishing House, 1982.

Truong, Ngo Quang. *The Easter Offensive of 1972.* Washington, DC: U.S. Army Center of Military History, 1980.

Tse-Tung, Mao. *On Guerilla Warfare.* Translated by Samuel Griffith. Eastford, CT: Martino Fine Books, 2017.

Van Nhut, Tran, and Christian Arevian. *An Loc: The Unfinished War.* Lubbock, TX: Texas Tech University Press, 2009.

Viet, Ha Mai. *Steel and Blood: South Vietnamese Armor and the War for Southeast Asia.* Annapolis, MD: Naval Institute Press, 2008.

Primary Sources (Unpublished)

Cold War International History Project (Wilson Center Digital Archive)

"Cable from the Chinese Embassy in Hungary, 'Please Inform Us of the Appropriate Attitude towards the Hungarian Events'," October 28, 1956, Wilson Center Digital Archive, PRC FMA 109–1041–01, 36. Obtained by Péter Vámos, translated by Péter Vámos and Gwenyth A. Jones. https://digitalarchive.wilsoncenter.org/document/119974.

"Cable from the Chinese Embassy in the Soviet Union, 'Recent Responses from the Soviet Revisionists to the Situation in Vietnam'," April 10, 1965, Wilson Center Digital Archive, PRC FMA 109–03654–02, 9–12. Translated by David Cowhig. https://digitalarchive.wilsoncenter.org/document/118725.

"Cable No. 10/TT.75, KBN [COSVN] Party Current Affairs Committee Circular," April 22, 1975, Wilson Center Digital Archive, *Dai Thang Mua Xuan, 1975: Van Kien Dang* [Great Spring Victory, 1975: Party Documents] (Hanoi: Nha xuat ban Chinh tri quoc gia, 2005), 302–4. Translated by Merle Pribbenow. https://digitalarchive.wilsoncenter.org/document/176150.

"Cable No. 38B from Brother Chien [Vo Nguyen Giap] to Brother Tuan [Van Tien Dung]," March 22, 1975, Wilson Center Digital Archive, *Dai Thang Mua Xuan, 1975: Van Kien Dang* [Great Spring Victory, 1975: Party Documents] (Hanoi: Nha xuat ban Chinh tri quoc gia, 2005), 166–67. Translated by Merle Pribbenow. https://digitalarchive.wilsoncenter.org/document/175988.

"Discussion between Chen Yi and Le Duc Tho," October 17, 1968, Wilson Center Digital Archive, CWIHP Working Paper 22, "77 Conversations." https://digitalarchive.wilsoncenter.org/document/112180.

"Discussion between Mao Zedong and Le Duan," September 24, 1975, Wilson Center Digital Archive, CWIHP Working Paper 22, "77 Conversations." https://digitalarchive.wilsoncenter.org/document/111263.

"Discussion between Zhou Enlai and Le Duan," March 23, 1966, Wilson Center Digital Archive, CWIHP Working Paper 22, "77 Conversations." https://digitalarchive.wilsoncenter.org/document/113069.

"Discussion between Zhou Enlai and Le Duan," July 13, 1971, Wilson Center Digital Archive, CWIHP Working Paper 22, "77 Conversations." https://digitalarchive.wilsoncenter.org/document/113109.

"Discussion between Zhou Enlai, Le Duan, and Pham Van Dong," March 7, 1971, Wilson Center Digital Archive, CWIHP Working Paper 22, "77 Conversations." https://digitalarchive.wilsoncenter.org/document/113108.

"Discussion between Zhou Enlai and Pham Van Dong," October 9, 1965, Wilson Center Digital Archive, CWIHP Working Paper 22, "77 Conversations." https://digitalarchive.wilsoncenter.org/document/113065.

"Joint Communique between the United States and China," February 27, 1972, Wilson Center Digital Archive, Nixon Presidential Library and Museum, Staff

Member Office Files (SMOF), President's Personal Files (PPF), Box 73. https://digitalarchive.wilsoncenter.org/document/121325.

"Khrushchev's Secret Speech, 'On the Cult of Personality and Its Consequences,' Delivered at the Twentieth Party Congress of the Communist Party of the Soviet Union," February 25, 1956, Wilson Center Digital Archive, From the Congressional Record: Proceedings and Debates of the 84th Congress, 2nd Session (May 22, 1956–June 11, 1956), C11, Part 7 (June 4, 1956), 9389–403. https://digitalarchive.wilsoncenter.org/document/115995.

"Mao Zedong's Talk at a Meeting of the Central Cultural Revolution Group (Excerpt)," March 15, 1969, Wilson Center Digital Archive, Zhonghua renmin gongheguo shilu [A Factual History of the People's Republic of China] (Changchun: Jilin renmin chubanshe, 1994), vol. 3, part 1, 467–69. https://digitalarchive.wilsoncenter.org/document/111241.

"Memorandum of Conversation from the Meeting between Premier Zhou Enlai and the Algerian Ambassador to China Mohamed Yala," August 6, 1964, Wilson Center Digital Archive, PRC FMA 106–01448–02, 98–117. Translated by Jake Tompkins. https://digitalarchive.wilsoncenter.org/document/118723.

"Minutes of Conversation between Ion Gheorghe Maurer, Paul Niculescu Mizil, Zhou Enlai, and Li Xiannian on 7 September 1969," September 7, 1969, Wilson Center Digital Archive, A.N.I.C., fond CC of RCP—External Relations Division, file 72/1969, 4–30. Published in Relatiile Romano-Chineze, 1880–1974 [Sino-Romanian Relations, 1880–1974], edited by Ioan Romulus Budura, (Bucharest, 2005), 943–59. Translated by Madalina Cristoloveanu. https://digitalarchive.wilsoncenter.org/document/117758.

"Minutes of Conversation, Mao Zedong and Ambassador Yudin," July 22, 1958, Wilson Center Digital Archive, Mao Zedong waijiao wenxuan [Selected Works of Mao Zedong on Diplomacy], Beijing: Zhongyang wenxian chubanshe, 1994, 322–33. Translated and annotated by Zhang Shu Guang and Chen Jian. https://digitalarchive.wilsoncenter.org/document/116982.

"Note No. 2/65 on Conversations with Comrade Shcherbakov about the Developmental Tendencies in the Democratic Republic of Vietnam, on 22 and 28 December 1964," January 6, 1965, Wilson Center Digital Archive, SAPMO-BArch, DY 30/IV A 2/20/442, 8–10. Translated from German by Lorenz Lüthi. https://digitalarchive.wilsoncenter.org/document/117710.

"Politburo Resolution No. 236-NQ/TW," August 13, 1974, Wilson Center Digital Archive, Dang Cong san Viet Nam, Van Kien Dang Toan tap [Party Documents Complete Series], vol. 35 (Hanoi: Nha xuat ban Chinh tri quoc gia, 2004), 116–23. Translated by Merle Pribbenow. https://digitalarchive.wilsoncenter.org/document/175861.

"Record of Conversation between Polish Delegation (Gomułka et al.) and Chinese Communist Politburo Member Liu Shaoqi, Moscow," November 20, 1960, Wilson Center Digital Archive, Sygnatura XI A15, KC PZPR, AAN, Warsaw. Obtained by Douglas Selvage and translated by Malgorzata Gnoinska. https://digitalarchive.wilsoncenter.org/document/117782.

"Record of Conversation from Premier Zhou's receiving of the Hungarian Ambassador to China Ágoston Szkladán on his Farewell Visit," November 2, 1956, Wilson Center Digital Archive, PRC FMA 109–01038–02, 1–10. Translated by Péter Vámos and Gwenyth A. Jones. https://digitalarchive.wilsoncenter.org/document/117695.

"Report by Four Chinese Marshals, Chen Yi, Ye Jianying, Nie Rongzhen, and Xu Xiangqian, to the Central Committee, 'Our Views about the Current Situation' (Excerpt)," September 17, 1969, Wilson Center Digital Archive, Zhonggong dangshi ziliao, no. 42 (June 1992), 84–86. Translated for CWIHP by Chen Jian with assistance from Li Di. https://digitalarchive.wilsoncenter.org/document/117154.

"Report from the Foreign Visitors Office of the Foreign Cultural Liaison Committee, 'The Two Major Parties of China and the Soviet Union Have Some Different Opinions, and Vietnam Faces Difficulties'," October 4, 1961, Wilson Center Digital Archive, PRC FMA 106–00661–01. Translated by Qingfei Yin. https://digitalarchive.wilsoncenter.org/document/120600.

"Report, 'My Observations on the Soviet Union,' Zhou Enlai to Mao Zedong and the Central Leadership (Excerpt)," January 24, 1957, Wilson Center Digital Archive, Shi Zhongquan, Zhou Enlai de zhuoyue fengxian [Remarkable Achievements and Contributions of Zhou Enlai] (Beijing: Zhonggong zhongyang dangxiao chubanshe, 1993), 302–5. Translated by Zhang Shu Guang and Chen Jian. https://digitalarchive.wilsoncenter.org/document/117033.

"Resolution of the 21st Plenum of the Party Central Committee, No. 227-NQ/TW (Excerpts)," October 13, 1973, Wilson Center Digital Archive, Dang Cong san Viet Nam, Van Kien Dang Toan tap [Party Documents Complete Series], vol. 34 (Hanoi: Nha xuat ban Chinh tri quoc gia, 2004), 210–261. Translated by Merle Pribbenow. https://digitalarchive.wilsoncenter.org/document/175857.

"Summary, Zhou Enlai's presentation at a meeting of the Chinese, Soviet, and Vietnamese delegations," June 15, 1954, Wilson Center Digital Archive, Zhou Enlai nianpu, 1949–1976, vol. 1, 383–84. Translated for CWIHP by Chen Jian. https://digitalarchive.wilsoncenter.org/document/121153.

"Telegram, Mao Zedong to Liu Shaoqi," January 17, 1950, Wilson Center Digital Archive, https://digitalarchive.wilsoncenter.org/document/112657.

"Telegram, Mao Zedong to Peng Dehuai and Huang Kecheng," April 28, 1954, Wilson Center Digital Archive, Mao wengao, vol. 5, 90. Translated for CWIHP by Chen Jian. https://digitalarchive.wilsoncenter.org/document/121145.

"Telegram, Zhou Enlai to Mao Zedong, Liu Shaoqi and the CCP Central Committee, 'A Brief Report on the Meetings at Liuzhou'," July 4, 1954, Wilson Center Digital Archive, PRC FMA 206–00049–03. Translated by Chen Zhihong. https://digitalarchive.wilsoncenter.org/document/111058.

"Telegram, Zhou Enlai to Mao Zedong, Liu Shaoqi, and the CCP Central Committee, Regarding the final plenary session of the conference (excerpt)," July 22, 1954,

Wilson Center Digital Archive, PRC FMA 206-Y0051. Translated by Chen Jian. https://digitalarchive.wilsoncenter.org/document/121168.

"The Polyansky Report on Khrushchev's Mistakes in Foreign Policy, October 1964," October 1964, Wilson Center Digital Archive, Library of Congress, Manuscript Division, Dmitriĭ Antonovich Volkogonov papers, 1887–1995, mm97083838, Reel 18. Translated by Svetlana Savranskaya, The National Security Archive. https://digitalarchive.wilsoncenter.org/document/115108.

"Transcript, Ho Chi Minh's presentation at the Liuzhou Conference (excerpt)," July 5, 1954, Wilson Center Digital Archive, Xiong Huayuan, Zhou Enlai chudeng shije wutai, 143–44. Translated for CWIHP by Chen Jian. https://digitalarchive.wilsoncenter.org/document/121160.

"Working Notes from the Session of the CPSU CC Presidium on 20 October 1956," October 20, 1956, Wilson Center Digital Archive, TsKhSD, F. 3, Op. 12, D. 1005, Ll. 49–50, compiled by V. N. Malin. Published in CWIHP Bulletin 8–9, 388. https://digitalarchive.wilsoncenter.org/document/111877.

"Zhou Enlai's Discussion with a Kenyan African National Federation Delegation (Excerpt)," September 5, 1963, Wilson Center Digital Archive, Dang de wenxian [Party Historical Documents], no. 3 (1994): 15–16. Translated by Neil Silver. https://digitalarchive.wilsoncenter.org/document/114355.

"Zhou Enlai Talking to Ho Chi Minh," March 1, 1965, Wilson Center Digital Archive, CWIHP Working Paper 22, "77 Conversations." https://digitalarchive.wilsoncenter.org/document/113055.

Foreign Relations of the United States

Foreign Relations of the United States, 1964–1968, vol. 1, Vietnam, 1964, eds. Edward Keefer and Charles Sampson (Washington, DC: Government Printing Office, 1992), Document 278.

Foreign Relations of the United States, 1964–1968, vol. 1, Vietnam, 1964, eds. Edward Keefer and Charles Sampson (Washington, DC: Government Printing Office, 1992), Document 295.

Foreign Relations of the United States, 1964–1968, vol. 1, Vietnam, 1964, eds. Edward Keefer and Charles Sampson (Washington, DC: Government Printing Office, 1992), Document 302.

Foreign Relations of the United States, 1969–1976, vol. 9, Vietnam, October 1972–January 1973, eds. John Carland and Edward Keefer (Washington, DC: Government Printing Office, 2010), Document 168.

Foreign Relations of the United States, 1969–1976, vol. 9, Vietnam, October 1972–January 1973, eds. John Carland and Edward Keefer, (Washington, DC: Government Printing Office, 2010), Document 206.

Foreign Relations of the United States, 1969–1976, vol. 7, Vietnam, July 1970–72, eds. David Goldman and Erin Mahan (Washington, DC: Government Printing Office, 2010), Document 170.

Foreign Relations of the United States, 1969–1976, vol. 12, Soviet Union, January 1969–October 1970, eds. Erin Mahan and Edward Keefer (Washington, DC: Government Printing Office, 2010), Document 14.

Foreign Relations of the United States, 1969–1976, vol. 13, Soviet Union, October 1970–October 1971, eds David Geyer and Edward C. Keefer (Washington, DC: Government Printing Office, 2011), Document 309.

Foreign Relations of the United States, 1969–1976, vol. 17, China, 1969–72, eds. Stephen E. Phillips and Edward C. Keefer (Washington, DC: Government Printing Office, 2010), Document 104.

Foreign Relations of the United States, 1969–1976, vol. 17, China, 1969–72, eds. Stephen E. Phillips and Edward C. Keefer (Washington, DC: Government Printing Office, 2010), Document 105.

Foreign Relations of the United States, 1969–1976, vol. 17, China, 1969–72, eds. Stephen E. Phillips and Edward C. Keefer (Washington, DC: Government Printing Office, 2010), Document 139.

Foreign Relations of the United States, 1977–1980, vol. 22, Southeast Asia and the Pacific, eds. David P. Nickles and Melissa Jane Taylor (Washington, DC: Government Printing Office, 2017), Document 41.

Freedom of Information Act Electronic Reading Room

"COMMUNIST MILITARY AND ECONOMIC AID TO NORTH VIETNAM, 1970–1974." Central Intelligence Agency, 1975. Freedom of Information Act Electronic Reading Room. https://www.cia.gov/readingroom/document/0001166499.

"NIE 53/14.3–1–74 THE LIKELIHOOD OF A MAJOR NORTH VIETNAMESE OFFENSIVE AGAINST SOUTH VIETNAM." Central Intelligence Agency, May 23, 1974. Freedom of Information Act Electronic Reading Room. https://www.cia.gov/readingroom/document/0001166463.

ProQuest Historical Newspaper Database

Kraslow, David. "Nixon Will Visit Moscow in May: Summit Talks to Review 'all Major Issues' MOSCOW TALKS." *Los Angeles Times*, October 13, 1971, 3-a1. https://www.proquest.com/historical-newspapers/nixon-will-visit-moscow-may/docview/156806221/se-2.

Morris, John. Special to the *New York Times*. "NIXON IS REVEALED AS AUTHOR OF STIR OVER INDO-CHINA: VICE PRESIDENT TOLD EDITORS U.S. MIGHT INTERVENE WITH TROOPS IF THE FRENCH QUIT TRIAL BALLOON IS SEEN STATE DEPARTMENT DECLARES IT IS 'HIGHLY UNLIKELY' FORCE WILL BE SENT TO ASIA NIXON CAUSED STIR OVER INDO-CHINA." The *New York Times*, April 18, 1954. https://www.proquest.com/historical-newspapers/nixon-is-revealed-as-author-stir-over-indo-china/docview/113095706/se-2.

Young, Robert. "HIGHT OFFICIAL HINTS OF WAR: WE MUST STOP REDS IN INDO-CHINA, HE SAYS CITES 'OBLIGATION' IF FRENCH QUIT FIGHTING." *Chicago Daily Tribune*, April 17, 1954. https://www.proquest.com/historical-newspapers/hight-official-hints-war/docview/178674379/se-2.

Texas Tech University Virtual Vietnam Archive

Assessment of Ho Chi Minh Trail Operation: March–April 1971, 2122004034. April 10, 1971, Box 20, Folder 04, Douglas Pike Collection: Unit 01—Assessment and Strategy, Vietnam Center and Sam Johnson Vietnam Archive, Texas Tech University, https://www.vietnam.ttu.edu/virtualarchive/items.php?item=2122004034.

"CHECO Reports #135; Lam Son 719 The South Vietnamese Incursion into Laos; 30 Jan–24 Mar 1971; 24 Mar 1971," 0390109001. March 24, 1971, Box 01, Folder 09, Contemporary Historical Examination of Current Operations (CHECO) Reports of Southeast Asia (1961–75), Vietnam Center and Sam Johnson Vietnam Archive, Texas Tech University, https://www.vietnam.ttu.edu/virtualarchive/items.php?item=0390109001.

"Combat After Action Report—Battle of Lang Vei, 5th Special Forces Group (Airborne). 1st Special Forces, Period 24 January–7 February 1968 (U)—U.S. Army," 1071806001. August 12, 1968, Box 18, Folder 06, Glenn Helm Collection, Vietnam Center and Sam Johnson Vietnam Archive, Texas Tech University, https://www.vietnam.ttu.edu/virtualarchive/items.php?item=1071806001.

Conflict studies: North Vietnam's blitzkrieg, 2131903007. Vietnam Center and Sam Johnson Vietnam Archive. Undated, Box 19, Folder 03, Douglas Pike Collection: Unit 02—Military Operations, Vietnam Center and Sam Johnson Vietnam Archive, Texas Tech University, https://www.vietnam.ttu.edu/virtualarchive/items.php?item=2131903007.

Determined to Completely Defeat the Enemy During the Nguyen Hue Campaign, 2122302014. Vietnam Center and Sam Johnson Vietnam Archive. 01 April 1972, Box 23, Folder 02, Douglas Pike Collection: Unit 01—Assessment and Strategy, Vietnam Center and Sam Johnson Vietnam Archive, Texas Tech University, https://www.vietnam.ttu.edu/virtualarchive/items.php?item=2122302014.

Grasp the Strategic Opportunity, 2122304036. Vietnam Center and Sam Johnson Vietnam Archive. April 1972, Box 23, Folder 04, Douglas Pike Collection: Unit 01—Assessment and Strategy, Vietnam Center and Sam Johnson Vietnam Archive, Texas Tech University, https://www.vietnam.ttu.edu/virtualarchive/items.php?item=2122304036.

Hanoi's 15th Plenum resolution—May 1959 by Tai Sung An, 23130010009. January 1, 1959, Box 30, Folder 010, Douglas Pike Collection: Unit 05—National Liberation Front, Vietnam Center and Sam Johnson Vietnam Archive, Texas Tech University, https://www.vietnam.ttu.edu/virtualarchive/items.php?item=23130010009.

History Of Vietnam 1954–1960: Evolution Of The War And Origins Of The Insurgency, 2321618001. 1958, Box 16, Folder 18, Douglas Pike Collection: Unit 06—Democratic Republic of Vietnam, Vietnam Center and Sam Johnson Vietnam Archive, Texas Tech University, https://www.vietnam.ttu.edu/virtualarchive/items.php?item=2321618001.

Infiltration Routes Used By PAVN Tanks To Penetrate The Quang Tri Battlefield And Organization And Activities Of The 203rd PAVN Armored Regiment, 2321317003. Vietnam Center and Sam Johnson Vietnam Archive. April 9, 1972, Box 13, Folder 17, Douglas Pike Collection: Unit 06—Democratic Republic of Vietnam, Vietnam Center and Sam Johnson Vietnam Archive, Texas Tech University, https://www.vietnam.ttu.edu/virtualarchive/items.php?item=2321317003.

Information On The Activities Of The 2nd And 12th Companies, 1st Battalion, 203rd Armored Regiment, In B3 Front, 2321317006. Vietnam Center and Sam Johnson Vietnam Archive. June 3, 1972, Box 13, Folder 17, Douglas Pike Collection: Unit 06—Democratic Republic of Vietnam, Vietnam Center and Sam Johnson Vietnam Archive, Texas Tech University, https://www.vietnam.ttu.edu/virtualarchive/items.php?item=2321317006.

Information On The 2nd T54 Tank Company, 1st Battalion, 203rd PAVN Armored Regiment, Participating In Combat On The Kontum City Front, 2321317004. Vietnam Center and Sam Johnson Vietnam Archive. May 18, 1972, Box 13, Folder 17, Douglas Pike Collection: Unit 06—Democratic Republic of Vietnam, Vietnam Center and Sam Johnson Vietnam Archive, Texas Tech University, https://www.vietnam.ttu.edu/virtualarchive/items.php?item=2321317004.

Memo from Moncrieff J. Spear, Consul General, Nha Trang to Ambassador Graham Martin—The Communist Offensive in Region Two—Part 1 of 2, 10840101003. [Ca. April 1975], Box 01, Folder 01, Moncrieff J. Spear Collection, Vietnam Center and Sam Johnson Vietnam Archive, Texas Tech University, https://www.vietnam.ttu.edu/virtualarchive/items.php?item=10840101003.

Memo from Senior Advisor 3rd VNMC Marine Infantry Battalion to Senior Marine Advisor—re: Evaluation of PAVN Easter '72 Offensive, 24991909035. Undated, Box 19, Folder 09, Dale W. Andrade Collection, Vietnam Center and Sam Johnson Vietnam Archive, Texas Tech University, https://www.vietnam.ttu.edu/virtualarchive/items.php?item=24991909035.

Message from John Vann to Creighton Abrams—re: Daily Commander's Evaluation, May 26, 1972, 24992403013. Undated, Box 24, Folder 3, Dale W. Andrade Collection, Vietnam Center and Sam Johnson Vietnam Archive, Texas Tech University, https://www.vietnam.ttu.edu/virtualarchive/items.php?item=24992403013.

North Vietnam's Doctrine, 2322504003. September 23, 1964, Box 25, Folder 04, Douglas Pike Collection: Unit 06—Democratic Republic of Vietnam, Vietnam Center and Sam Johnson Vietnam Archive, Texas Tech University, https://www.vietnam.ttu.edu/virtualarchive/items.php?item=2322504003.

Operational Analyses, Rand Corporation—Giap and the Seventh Son—re: Analysis of General Giap's Spring Offensive, 24991810003. Vietnam Center and Sam Johnson

Vietnam Archive. Undated, Box 18, Folder 10, Dale W. Andrade Collection, Vietnam Center and Sam Johnson Vietnam Archive, Texas Tech University, https://www.vietnam.ttu.edu/virtualarchive/items.php?item=24991810003.

PRGRSV Spokesman Accuses U.S., RVN of Cease-Fire Violations—Paris AFP, 2132210046. February 12, 1973, Box 22, Folder 10, Douglas Pike Collection: Unit 02—Military Operations, Vietnam Center and Sam Johnson Vietnam Archive, Texas Tech University, https://www.vietnam.ttu.edu/virtualarchive/items.php?item=2132210046.

PAVN Memorandum on Failure to Capture An Loc: May 1972—re: Nguyen Hue Campaign, 2122401007. Vietnam Center and Sam Johnson Vietnam Archive. May 1972, Box 24, Folder 01, Douglas Pike Collection: Unit 01—Assessment and Strategy, Vietnam Center and Sam Johnson Vietnam Archive, Texas Tech University, https://www.vietnam.ttu.edu/virtualarchive/items.php?item=2122401007.

Quan Doi Nhan Dan on PLAF Successes in 1971, 2122010053. July 30, 1971, Box 20, Folder 10, Douglas Pike Collection: Unit 01—Assessment and Strategy, Vietnam Center and Sam Johnson Vietnam Archive, Texas Tech University, https://www.vietnam.ttu.edu/virtualarchive/items.php?item=2122010053.

"Report, Briefing Material—re: Review of PAVN Armor Tactics and Training—Record of MACV Part 2," F015900190228. Vietnam Center and Sam Johnson Vietnam Archive. November 8, 1972, Box 0019, Folder 0228, Sam Johnson Vietnam Archive Collection, Vietnam Center and Sam Johnson Vietnam Archive, Texas Tech University, https://www.vietnam.ttu.edu/virtualarchive/items.php?item=F015900190228.

"Report, Intelligence Directorate—The Nguyen-Hue Offensive—Record of MACV Part 1," F015800210009. Vietnam Center and Sam Johnson Vietnam Archive. January 12, 1973, Box 0021, Folder 0009, Sam Johnson Vietnam Archive Collection, Vietnam Center and Sam Johnson Vietnam Archive, Texas Tech University, https://www.vietnam.ttu.edu/virtualarchive/items.php?item=F015800210009.

"Report, MACV J2—The Tank Battles at Dong Ha—re: 20th ARVN Tank Regiment battles," 24991908009. Vietnam Center and Sam Johnson Vietnam Archive. Undated, Box 19, Folder 08, Dale W. Andrade Collection, Vietnam Center and Sam Johnson Vietnam Archive, Texas Tech University, https://www.vietnam.ttu.edu/virtualarchive/items.php?item=24991908009.

"Report, United States Military Assistance Command Vietnam—Lao Dong Central Committee Resolutions 1965–69," 1071326005. 1970, Box 13, Folder 26, Glenn Helm Collection, Vietnam Center and Sam Johnson Vietnam Archive, Texas Tech University, https://www.vietnam.ttu.edu/virtualarchive/items.php?item=1071326005.

Revolts And Repressions, 2320724002. 1956, Box 07, Folder 24, Douglas Pike Collection: Unit 06—Democratic Republic of Vietnam, Vietnam Center and Sam Johnson Vietnam Archive, Texas Tech University, https://www.vietnam.ttu.edu/virtualarchive/items.php?item=2320724002.

Study Of Military Information On The 5th Battalion, 203rd Armored Regiment, PAVN Armor Command, On The An Loc Battlefield, 2321317001. Vietnam

Center and Sam Johnson Vietnam Archive. April 13, 1972, Box 13, Folder 17, Douglas Pike Collection: Unit 06—Democratic Republic of Vietnam, Vietnam Center and Sam Johnson Vietnam Archive, Texas Tech University, https://www.vietnam.ttu.edu/virtualarchive/items.php?item=2321317001.

"Translated Report—re: On the Final Analysis of Offensive Operations in South Vietnam and Requirements for the future Armed Struggle," 11271625003. Vietnam Center and Sam Johnson Vietnam Archive. July 2, 1993, Box 16, Folder 25, Garnett Bell Collection, Vietnam Center and Sam Johnson Vietnam Archive, Texas Tech University, https://www.vietnam.ttu.edu/virtualarchive/items.php?item=11271625003.

Working Paper—The Power Struggle in North Vietnam, 24991810007. Vietnam Center and Sam Johnson Vietnam Archive. Undated, Box 18, Folder 10, Dale W. Andrade Collection, Vietnam Center and Sam Johnson Vietnam Archive, Texas Tech University, https://www.vietnam.ttu.edu/virtualarchive/items.php?item=24991810007.

The United States of America Vietnam War Commemoration

Galloway, Joseph. Interview with Dennis Thompson, Army, October 17, 2018. The United States of American Vietnam War Commemoration. https://www.vietnam-war50th.com/history_and_legacy/oral_history/thompson,-dennis/.

Secondary Sources

Andradé, Dale. *Trail By Fire: The 1972 Easter Offensive, America's Last Vietnam Battle.* New York: Hippocrene Books, 1995.

Andrew, Christopher, and Vasili Mitrokhin. *The World Was Going Our Way: The KGB and the Battle for the Third World.* New York, NY: Basic Books, 2005.

Asselin, Pierre. *Vietnam's American War: A History.* Cambridge, UK: Cambridge University Press, 2018.

Berman, Larry. *No Peace, No Honor: Nixon, Kissinger, & Betrayal in Vietnam.* New York: The Free Press, 2001.

Cash, John, John Albright, and Allan Sandstrum. *Seven Firefights in Vietnam.* Mineola, NY: Dover Publications, 2007.

Chen, Jian. *Mao's China and the Cold War.* Chapel Hill, NC: University of North Carolina Press, 2001.

Cooper, John. "The Sino-Vietnam War's Thirtieth Anniversary." *American Journal of Chinese Studies* 16, no. 1 (April 2009): 71–74.

Daddis, Gregory. *Withdrawal: Reassessing America's Final Years in Vietnam.* New York, NY: Oxford University Press, 2017.

Dikötter, Frank. *Mao's Great Famine: The History of China's Most Devastating Catastrophe, 1958–1962.* London: Bloomsbury Publishing, 2010.

———. *The Cultural Revolution: A People's History, 1962–1976.* New York, NY: Bloomsbury Publishing, 2019.

Duiker, William. "Waging Revolutionary War: The Evolution of Hanoi's Strategy in the South, 1959–1965." In *The Vietnam War: Vietnamese and American Perspectives.* Armonk, NY: M.E. Sharpe, 1993.

Dunstan, Simon. *Vietnam Tracks: Armor in Battle 1945–1975.* Novato, CA: Presidio Press, 1982.

Elleman, Bruce. *Modern Chinese Warfare. 1795–1989.* London: Routledge, 2001.

Friedman, Jeremy. *Shadow Cold War: The Sino-Soviet Competition for the Third World.* Chapel Hill, NC: University of North Carolina Press, 2015.

Gaiduk, Ilya. *Confronting Vietnam: Soviet Policy toward the Indochina Conflict 1954–1963.* Washington, DC: Woodrow Wilson Center Press, 2003.

———. *The Soviet Union and the Vietnam War.* Chicago: Ivan R. Dee, 1996.

Girling, J. L. S. *People's War: Conditions and Consequences in China and South East Asia.* New York, NY: Frederick A. Praeger, 1969.

Goscha, Christopher. "Vietnam, the Third Indochina War and the Meltdown of Asian Internationalism." In *The Third Indochina War: Conflict between China, Vietnam, and Cambodia, 1972–79*, edited by Odd Arne Westad and Sophie Quinn-Judge. London: Routledge, 2006.

Hastings, Max. *Vietnam: An Epic Tragedy 1945–1975.* London: William Collins, 2018.

Hughes, Ken. *Fatal Politics: The Nixon Tapes, The Vietnam War, and the Casualties of Reelection.* Charlottesville, VA: University of Virginia Press, 2015.

Isaacs, Arnold. *Without Honor: Defeat in Vietnam and Cambodia.* Baltimore, MD: The Johns Hopkins University Press, 1983.

Khoo, Nicholas. *Collateral Damage: Sino-Soviet Rivalry and the Termination of the Sino-Vietnamese Alliance.* New York, NY: Columbia University Press, 2011.

Kiernan, Ben. *Blood and Soil: A World History of Genocide and Extermination from Sparta to Darfur.* New Haven, CT: Yale University Press, 2007.

———. *The Pol Pot Regime: Race, Power, and Genocide in Cambodia under the Khmer Rouge, 1975–79.* Third Edition. New Haven, CT: Yale University Press, 2008.

Logevall, Fredrik. *Embers of War: The Fall of an Empire and the Making of America's Vietnam.* New York, NY: Random House, 2012.

Lüthi, Lorenzo. *The Sino-Soviet Split: Cold War in the Communist World.* Princeton, NJ: Princeton University Press, 2008.

McKenna, Thomas. *Kontum: The Battle to Save South Vietnam.* Lexington, KY: University Press of Kentucky, 2011.

McMaster, H. R. *Dereliction of Duty: Lyndon Johnson, Robert McNamara, the Joint Chiefs of Staff, and the Lies That Led to Vietnam.* New York, NY: Harper Perennial, 1997.

Morris, Stephen. *Why Vietnam Invaded Cambodia: Political Culture and the Causes of War.* Stanford, CA: Stanford University Press, 1999.

Nguyen, Lien-Hang. *Hanoi's War: An International History of the War for Peace in Vietnam.* Chapel Hill, NC: University of North Carolina Press, 2012.

O'Dowd, Edward. *Chinese Military Strategy in the Third Indochina War: The Last Maoist War.* London: Routledge, 2007.
Olsen, Mari. *Soviet–Vietnam Relations and the Role of China, 1949–64: Changing Alliances.* London: Routledge, 2006.
Phillips, William. *Night of the Silver Stars: The Battle of Lang Vei.* Annapolis, MD: Naval Institute Press, 1997.
Pike, Douglas. *Vietnam and the Soviet Union: Anatomy of An Alliance.* Boulder, CO: Westview Press, 1987.
Qiang, Zhai. *China and the Vietnam Wars, 1950–1975.* Chapel Hill, NC: University of North Carolina Press, 2000.
Quinn-Judge, Sophie. "Victory on the Battlefield; Isolation in Asia: Vietnam's Cambodia Decade, 1979–1989." In *The Third Indochina War: Conflict between China, Vietnam, and Cambodia, 1972–79*, edited by Odd Arne Westad and Sophie Quinn-Judge. London: Routledge, 2006.
Radchenko, Sergey. *Two Suns in the Heavens: The Sino-Soviet Struggle for Supremacy, 1962–1967.* Woodrow Wilson Center Press, 2009.
———. *Unwanted Visionaries: The Soviet Failure in Asia at the End of the Cold War.* New York, NY: Oxford University Press, 2014.
Randolph, Stephen. "A Bigger Game: Nixon, Kissinger, and the 1972 Easter Offensive." George Washington University, 2005.
———. *Powerful and Brutal Weapons: Nixon, Kissinger, and the Easter Offensive.* Cambridge, MA: Harvard University Press, 2007.
Rosser-Owen, David. *Vietnam Weapons Handbook.* Wellingborough, UK: Patrick Stephens Limited, 1986.
Service, Robert. *Comrades: A History of World Communism.* Cambridge, MA: Harvard University Press, 2010.
Starry, Donn. *Mounted Combat in Vietnam.* Washington, DC: Department of the Army, 1978.
Turley, G. H. *The Easter Offensive: Vietnam 1972.* Novato, CA: Presidio, 1985.
Veith, George. *Black April: The Fall of South Vietnam, 1973–75.* New York, NY: Encounter Books, 2013.
Viet, Ha Mai. *Steel and Blood: South Vietnamese Armor and the War for Southeast Asia.* Annapolis, MD: Naval Institute Press, 2008.
Westad, Odd Arne. *The Cold War: A World History.* London: Penguin Books, 2018.
Willbanks, James. *A Raid Too Far: Operation Lam Son 719 and Vietnamization in Laos.* College Station, TX: Texas A&M University Press, 2014.
———. *Abandoning Vietnam: How America Left and South Vietnam Lost Its War.* Lawrence, KS: University Press of Kansas, 2004.
———. *The Battle of An Loc.* Bloomington, IN: Indiana University Press, 2005.
Xiaobing, Li. *Building Ho's Army: Chinese Military Assistance to North Vietnam.* Lexington, KY: University Press of Kentucky, 2019.

———. *The Dragon in the Jungle: The Chinese Army in the Vietnam War*. New York, NY: Oxford University Press, 2020.

Xiaoming, Zhang. "Deng Xiaoping and China's Decision to Go to War with Vietnam." *Journal of Cold War Studies* 12, no. 3 (Summer 2010): 3–29.

Zubok, Vladislav. *A Failed Empire: The Soviet Union in the Cold War from Stalin to Gorbachev*. Chapel Hill, NC: University of North Carolina Press, 2009.

Index

Abrams, General Creighton, 53–54, 58
An Loc, xxii, 69–76, 79
   Battle of, 73
Anti-American Resistance for National Salvation, 40
Army
   11th Armored Cavalry, 57
   202nd Tank Regiment, 26, 55
   203rd Armored Regiment, 69–70
   304th Division, 55
   308th Division, 26, 55
   Army of the Republic of Vietnam (ARVN), xvii, xix–xx, 29, 40, 45–47, 51, 54–59, 70–79, 85, 89–91, 104
   French Army, 1
   Green Berets, 47–48, 50–51 *see also* U.S. Army Special Forces
   North Vietnamese Army (NVA), xxiv, 30
   People's Army of Vietnam (PAVN), xvii, xxiv, 21, 26–28, 30–31, 36, 39–41, 46–55, 57–59, 68–79, 83–92, 94–95, 98, 99, 103–5, 107–8, 110–12
   People's Liberation Armed Forces of Vietnam (PLAF), 25
   People's Liberation Army (PLA), 25, 101, 110–11
   Republic of Vietnam Armed Forces (South Vietnam) (RVNAF), xvii, 53–54
   South Vietnamese Regional/Popular Defense Forces (RF/PF), 71
   U.S. Army Special Forces, 47 *see also* Green Berets
Association of Southeast Asian Nations, 112

Ban Me Thout, 89–90
Beijing, xix–xxii, 9, 13, 16, 19, 22, 25, 27, 29, 34–39, 43–45, 59, 61–65, 67, 78, 86–87, 93–96, 99–100, 102, 105–9, 111–12
Berlin, 5, 65
   Blockade, 5
   West, 65
blitzkrieg, 79, 108
Brezhnev, Leonid, 36–38, 41, 44, 58, 62, 66, 84, 86, 94
Brzezinski, Zbigniew, 109
Buddhism, 29
Bunker, Ellsworth, 82

Cambodia, 7, 10–11, 14, 39, 54–55, 63, 68, 99, 102–9, 111–12
Camp Carroll, 72, 74
Cao Ba Lanh Mountain, 111
Carter, Jimmy, 109
Central Committee, 62–63, 85, 101, 107
Chennault, Anna, 81–82
Chen Yi, Commander, 67
Chiao Kuan Hua, 63

China *see* People's Republic of China (PRC)
Chinese Communist Party (CCP), 3–4, 16–20, 25, 38, 42, 45, 55, 62, 64, 100, 105–6, 109
Chinese Civil War, 15, 24, 92
Chinese Military Assistance Group (CMAG), 4–5, 11, 13–14, 92
Chinh, Truong, 21–22, 61
Civilian Irregular Defense Group (CIDG), 47, 51
Cogny, Major General René, 1–2
Combined Document Exploitation Center (CDEC), xxiii
communique, 7, 43, 65, 102
Communist Party of Kampuchea (CPK), 104
Communist Party of the Soviet Union (CPSU), 5, 15, 19–21, 32, 35–36, 42, 44
Cold War, xxi, xxii, xxiii, 8, 62, 65, 112
Cold War International History Project (CWIHP), xxiii
coup, 29, 66, 91, 104
Cuba, 20, 37
Cuban Missile Crisis, 19–20, 35
Cultural Revolution, 39, 42–45, 58, 61–62, 67, 94, 97, 100–102, 110
Czechoslovakia, 61

De Castries, Brigadier General Christian, 1–2, 6
Democratic Kampuchea (DK), 103
Democratic Party, 53, 81–82
Democratic Republic of Vietnam (DRV/North Vietnam), xxiv, 3–7, 10–14, 21–25, 27, 29–32, 35–38, 41, 44–45
Deng Xiaoping, 44, 99–100, 102, 108–9
Dien Bien Phu, 1–9, 11–13, 24, 30, 92–95
Diem, Ngo Dinh, 23, 29, 94
Dobrynin, Anatoly, 65

Dong Ha, xvii, xx, 70–73, 79, 98
Dong, Pham Van, 7, 10, 12, 22, 41–42, 44, 64, 101
Dung, General Van Tien, 84, 87, 89–90

Easter Offensive, xvii, xxi, 61, 64–79, 83, 85, 94, 104
Eden, Anthony, 12–13
Eisenhower administration, 8–9

Five-Year Plan, 8
Ford administration, xxiii, 88
Ford, Gerald, 87–89, 91–92
Foreign Relations of the U.S. (FRUS), xxiii
French War, 21

Gang of Four, 100
Geneva, 1, 6–14, 23–24, 27, 78, 93, 95
Geneva Accords, 12, 23–24, 93
Geneva Conference, xviii, 6, 8, 10, 12–13, 93
Giap, Vo Nguyen, 1, 11, 13, 30, 32, 44, 61, 68, 85, 89–90
Golikov, V. A., 37–38
Gorbachev, Mikhail, 112
"Grasp the Strategic Opportunity," 67
Great Leap Forward, 17–18, 21, 42, 102
Great Terror, 21
Guangxi province, 43–45
guerilla, xix, 4, 30, 55, 87
Gulf of Tonkin, xxi, 28, 29, 33–36, 94

Haig, Al, 83
Hanoi, xvii–xxi, 21–22, 25–28, 29–30, 32–37, 39–41, 43–47, 52, 58–59, 64, 66–68, 76, 81–82, 84–88, 91, 93–98, 99, 101–4, 106–9, 111–12
Harriman, Averill, 81
Highway 9, 47
Ho Chi Minh, xviii, 1–7, 10–11, 14, 19, 22, 24–25, 27, 30, 32, 40, 54, 67, 86, 92–94, 102

Hungary, 16–17, 93

imperialism, 14, 16, 18, 35, 41, 45, 62–63, 106
Indochina War
    First, xviii, xx, xxi, 1, 3, 5, 10, 22, 27
    Third, 108–11
Islam, 105

Jiang Jieshi, 2
Johnson, Lyndon, 33–36, 53, 81–82

Kang Sheng, 19–20
Korean War, 4, 9, 110
Khe Sanh, 46–48, 51
Khmer Rouge, 99, 102–8, 111
Khrushchev, Nikita, 12, 15–21, 27, 35–40, 42, 84, 93–94
Kissinger, Henry, 63–66, 82–83, 91
Kontum, xxii, 70, 75

Laird, Melvin, 53
Lang Vei, 45, 47–51, 54, 59, 94, 98
Laniel, Joseph, 10
Laos, 7, 10, 77, 82–83, 108
Le Duan, xix–xx, 13, 22–25, 28, 30–33, 36–37, 43–44, 46, 61, 64, 66–67, 85–88, 93, 99–102, 107, 112
Leninism, xix, 15, 18–19 *see also* Marxism-Leninism
Limited Test Ban Treaty, 20
Liu Shaoqi, 3–4, 16
Luom, Sergeant, xvii, 71–72, 98

Malinovskii, Rodion, 38
Maoism, 22, 27, 30, 41, 46, 59, 94, 102, 104, 110
Mao Zedong, xviii, xxi, 2–4, 7–8, 12–15, 19, 31; 35–36, 38, 41–44, 46, 58–59, 62, 64, 67, 86, 93–95, 97, 99–100, 102, 104, 110
Marine Combat Base, 47–48

Marxism, xix, 15, 18, 103
    -Leninism, xix, 15, 18
McCone, John A., 33–34
McNamara, Robert, 33
Mendès France, Pierre, 10–13
Military Assistance Command, Vietnam (MACV), 32, 53, 70, 77
Military Region (MR)
    -1, xvii, 70, 72, 74
    -3, 72, 74, 88
Moffett, Captain Hal, 74
Moscow, xviii, xx, xxii, 4–6, 9, 12–13, 16–17, 19–20, 25, 27, 29, 32, 34, 36–41, 44, 47, 61–67, 78, 85–86, 93–95, 97, 99, 101, 107, 109, 112
    Conference, 25, 32
Molotov, Vyacheslav, 7, 11, 13

National Intelligence Estimate (U.S.) (NIE), 87–88
National Liberation Front (NLF), xxiv, 24
National United Front of Cambodia (FUNK), 104
Navy, 33, 47, 54
    North Vietnamese naval vessels, 33
    South Vietnamese Navy (RVNN), xvi
    U.S. Navy fighter bombers, 33
Ngyuen Hue Offensive *see* Spring–Summer Offensive
Nguyen, Lien-Hang, xx, xxiii
Nixon administration, xvii, xxiii, 62–64, 66–67, 78, 82
Nixon, Richard, 9, 16, 53–54, 58, 61–67, 78, 81–84, 87–88, 95 *see also* Nixon administration, Watergate scandal
North Vietnamese Army (NVA), xxiv, 30 *see also* Viet Cong
nuclear, 19–20, 26, 30, 37

Operation *Lam Son 719*, 52, 54–55, 94

Paris, 64, 81–85, 87–88, 95
  Peace Accords, xxiv, 81–85, 87–88, 95
Peking *see* Beijing
People's Army of Vietnam (PAVN), xvii, xxiv, 21, 26–28, 30–31, 36, 39–41, 46–55, 57–59, 68–79, 83–92, 94–95, 98, 99, 103–5, 107–8, 110–12
  tankers, 68
People's Liberation Army (PLA), 25, 101, 110–11
People's Liberation Armed Forces of Vietnam (PLAF), 25
People's Republic of China (PRC), xviii–xix, 2–10, 12–27, 31, 33–46, 58, 61–67, 86, 92–95, 97, 99–100, 102, 106–9, 112
Phan Rang, 91
Phnom Penh, 103–6, 108
Phuoc Long, 87–89, 95
Podgorny, Nikolai, 68
Poland, 16–17, 93
policymaker, xviii, 27, 36
Politburo (Soviet), 14, 16, 36–37, 76
Politburo (Vietnamese), xvii, xix, 21–24, 27, 30, 32, 46, 58–59, 61, 69, 78, 81, 85, 87, 90, 93, 107–9, 111–12
  11th Plenum, 23
  15th Plenum, 23–24, 28, 30
  21st Plenum, 85–86
Polyansky Report, 37
Pot, Pol, 103–6, 111

Quang, Lieutenant General Tran Van, 75–76
Quang Ninh, 111
Quang Tri, 72, 79

Red Guards, 42–43, 45
Republic of Vietnam (South Vietnam) (RVN), 3, 12, 14, 92 *see also* Democratic Republic of Vietnam (DRV/North Vietnam)
Republic of Vietnam Armed Forces (South Vietnam) (RVNAF), xvii, 53–54
Resist America and Assist Vietnam Movement, 35
Resolution 9, 30–34, 40, 59
Revisionist Anti-Party Affair, 32
Romania, 62

Saigon, xx, 25, 29–30, 33, 78–79, 81–83, 85, 87, 89–93, 95, 99, 101–2, 106–7
  fall of, xx, xxiv, 81–97, 99, 102, 106–7
Secret Speech, 15–17
Seven Thousand Cadres Conference, 42
Sharp, Admiral Ulysses, 33
Shcherbakov, Ilia, 39
Sihanouk, Norodom, 103–4
Sino-Soviet border, 62, 65
Sino-Soviet split, xviii–xxiii, 14, 23, 31, 93, 97
Sokolovsky, Marshal V. D., xix
South Vietnamese Regional/Popular Defense Forces (RF/PF), 71
Soviet Union, xviii, xxi, xxiii, xxiv, 2–7, 12–23, 27, 32–33, 35–42, 44–45, 58, 62, 66, 68–69, 83, 88, 93–94, 99, 101, 107, 109–10, 112 *see also* USSR
Special Forces camp (U.S.), 47, 49, 51–52
Spring–Summer Offensive (1972), xvii, 68
Stalin, Josef, 2–6, 9, 14–16, 21, 27, 32, 93
Stepako, V. I., 37–38

Tactical Operations Center (TOC) bunker, 50–51
Tchepone, 54, 57, 59
Tet Offensive, xx, 45–48, 51, 81, 94
Thieu, Nguyen Van, 53, 57–58, 83, 90–92, 95

Tho, Le Duc, 22, 61, 67, 83
Thompson, Sergeant Major Dennis, 50
Tito, Josef Broz, 5, 19
Trapeznikov, Sergei, 37–38
Treaty of Friendship and Cooperation, 101, 108, 112
Truong, Lieutenant General Ngo Quang, 74–75

United Kingdom, 7, 20
Union of Soviet Socialist Republics (USSR), 12, 32, 41, 58, 68, 78 *see also* Soviet Union
USS *Enterprise*, 89
USS *Maddox*, 28, 33
USS *Ticonderoga*, 33
USS *Turner Joy*, 28, 33

Viet Cong (VC), xvii, xxiii, xxiv, 24, 36, 40–41, 46, 52–54, 71, 83, 92, 94, 103–4 *see also* North Vietnamese Army
Viet Minh, xviii, 1–7, 11, 92–93, 95, 104
Vietnamese Workers' Party (VWP), 13–14, 21, 23, 27–29, 31–32, 37
Third Congress, 25
Vietnamization, xvii, 46, 52–54, 59, 93
Vinh, 33

Warsaw Pact, 16, 18

Washington, DC, xix–xx, 33, 52, 58, 63–66, 81, 87, 109
Watergate scandal, 87 *see also* Nixon, Richard
weapons
  antiaircraft guns, 4
  High Explosive Anti-Tank (HEAT) rounds, 48
  M72 Light Anti-tank launcher, xvii, 48, 50, 72, 89
  machine gun, 29, 49
  nuclear arms, 19–20, 26, 30, 37
  PT-76, 26, 47, 49–52, 57, 59
  rifle, 45, 48, 50
  rocket, 47–48, 50, 57, 72, 74, 89, 92
  tank, xvii–xxii, 6, 26, 45, 47–52, 55–57, 59, 62, 68–79, 88, 96, 98, 99, 110–11 *see also* Tank 843
  Tank 843, 96, 98
  T-34, 26
Wei Guoqing, 4, 11
Wheeler, Earl, 53
White House, 33, 53–54, 81–82
Willoughby, Captain Frank, 48, 51
World War II, xiv, 26, 81

Year Zero, 102

Zhou Enlai, 5, 7–8, 10, 12–13, 17–18, 20, 34–35, 38, 40–45, 62–67, 99–100, 102